14769 (2) 10/6/75

GU00202092

BETWEEN 1939 and 1945 the life of every Englishman was geared to one aim: the defeat of Hitler. His existence was ordered by the state as never before. Under attack and from the fear of invasion the government felt bound to control personal liberty. Emergency powers, the direction of labour, the licensing system, rationing, enforced saving, security restrictions, the black-out, all minutely affected daily life.

Under this bureaucratic umbrella, the valiant efforts of air raid wardens, fire watchers, W.V.S. volunteers, became a wartime myth. Their criticisms of the shortages, anxiety and the break up of homes, are less well known. In 1939, those on the extreme left believed that the war could not be won without a social revolution. The two halves of the nation met when families were evacuated, when professional and worker together manned Civil Defence posts and when "Bevin boys" went down mines.

The war brought radical changes in English society, not revolution. The demands of the blitz highlighted the need for welfare. Evacuees and casualties showed up the defects of the housing, education and medical services. The new habit of state control led to planning for better and fairer living conditions. The welfare state itself grew out of the war.

Illustrated throughout with contemporary photographs, this addition to THE WAYLAND DOCUMENTARY HISTORY SERIES draws on diaries, political manifestoes, newspapers, journals, novelists and poets to provide a unique and graphic account of the English people in wartime.

Frontispiece overleaf   A London family gives the "Thumbs up" sign after sheltering from a German air raid

The Home Front

Britain 1939-45

Marion Yass

WAYLAND PUBLISHERS LONDON

Available in hardback (*limp edition also available):

THE VIKINGS   *Michael Gibson*
*MEDIEVAL PILGRIMS   *Alan Kendall*
THE BLACK DEATH AND PEASANTS' REVOLT   *Leonard Cowie*
*THE REFORMATION OF THE SIXTEENTH CENTURY   *Leonard Cowie*
THE PILGRIM FATHERS   *Leonard Cowie*
*WITCHCRAFT   *Roger Hart*
*PLAGUE AND FIRE   *Leonard Cowie*
*THE AGE OF DICKENS   *Patrick Rooke*
ENGLAND EXPECTS   *Roger Hart*
GLADSTONE AND DISRAELI   *Patrick Rooke*
*ORIGINS OF WORLD WAR ONE   *R. Parkinson*
THE GREAT DEPRESSION   *Marion Yass*
THE THIRD REICH   *Michael Berwick*
*ORIGINS OF WORLD WAR TWO   *R. Parkinson*
*THE HOME FRONT   *Marion Yass*
HIROSHIMA   *Marion Yass*
WOMEN'S RIGHTS   *Patrick Rooke*
THE COLD WAR   *Elisabeth Barker*
THE TRIAL AND EXECUTION OF CHARLES I   *Leonard Cowie*
BLACK CARGO   *Richard Howard*
THE RISE OF JAPAN   *Michael Gibson*
ITALY UNDER MUSSOLINI   *Christopher Leeds*
THE BRITISH RAJ   *Denis Judd*

SBN (hardback edition): 85340 154 3
SBN (limp edition): 85340 214 0
Second impression 1973
Copyright © 1971 by Wayland (Publishers) Ltd,
101 Grays Inn Road, London WC1
Printed in Great Britain by The Garden City Press Limited,
Letchworth, Hertfordshire SG6 1JS.

Contents

The Illustrations

1 Munich 1938

THE OUTBREAK of the Second World War came as no surprise to the British people. The signs in Adolf Hitler's Germany and Benito Mussolini's Italy were ominous. Early in 1938 Ernest Bevin warned: "Those who are building up their hopes upon some internal dissension breaking up regimes, and those who are hoping that war will be avoided by some miraculous happening, are building on sand. I have never believed from the first day when Hitler came to office but that he intended, at the right moment and when he was strong enough, to wage war in the world. Neither do I believe, with that kind of philosophy that there is any possibility to arrive at agreements with Hitler or Mussolini (1)."

Since 1933 Hitler had been strengthening his Nazi (National Socialist) dictatorship. When Mussolini forcibly annexed Abyssinia in 1935 he shattered the hope that the League of Nations could keep the peace, and that the First World War was indeed the war to end wars. The British people were less clear sighted about these signs than Bevin. They were just recovering from the worst of the Great Depression which followed the Wall Street Crash of 1929. Their life was very different from the frantic political activity in Germany. As George Orwell wrote, "It is somehow bound up with solid breakfasts and gloomy Sundays . . . the clatter of clogs in the Lancashire mill towns, the to-and-fro of lorries on the Great North Road, the queues outside the Labour Exchanges, the rattle of pin tables in the Soho pubs, the old maids biking to Holy Communion through the mists of the Autumn mornings . . . It is a land where the bus conductors are good tempered and the policemen carry no revolvers. In no country inhabited by white men is it easier to shove people off the pavement. And with this goes . . .

Facing page. Top "Peace with honour." Neville Chamberlain brings back the Munich Agreement made with Hitler in 1938. But peace was doomed. *Bottom* A German guard in Hitler-occupied Poland

the English hatred of war and militarism (2)."

Everybody wanted peace; they were reluctant to face the possibility of war. In March, 1938, Germany occupied Austria. Essex villagers "cocked an anxious eye at the government, but received no warning dig in the ribs from it. There was none of the time-honoured rumbling on the drums, no sudden reminder that the army was a man's life; nothing, only an insistence on social improvements at home which, as everybody knows, indicates an all-clear abroad (3)." Neville Chamberlain, the British Prime Minister since 1937, saw himself as a social reformer. His measures of economic planning had improved the living conditions of Britain in the thirties. He was nearly seventy and had no more desire for war than most other people. Rearmament was only gradually speeded up during his premiership.

British pacifism

At the beginning of September, 1939, a public opinion survey was held. It was one of the first of its kind. Organized by a team of journalists under the name Mass Observation, it found that only fifteen per cent of those questioned expected war. Fifty-five per cent said firmly there would be no war (4). Fears increased with Hitler's threat to Czechoslovakia. When Chamberlain flew to Godesberg to remonstrate, it seemed that he would agree to Hitler's demand for immediate German occupation of the Sudetan areas. A man interviewed at New Cross, London, gave a typical reaction: "I'm just a working class man and I'm as entitled to an opinion as anybody else. We've let them down good and proper (5)." The editor of the *Star* commented: "A deep yearning for peace is shot through by dismay at the humiliation of surrender. The country is in a ferment as never before (6)."

State of emergency

Sympathy for the Czechs evaporated as preparations brought home the reality of war. A journalist reported after Chamberlain's return that, "Throughout the country, yesterday was used to press on vigorously, though calmly, with preparations for passive defence in the event of an emergency ... In London protective trenches for use in air raids were dug in Hyde Park, St. James's Park and the Green Park, and workmen were busy in all three taking measurements and marking with stakes the sites for more of these shelters against blast and splinters ... Announcements on the screens at cinemas, from the stage at theatres, from the pulpit in churches, and at sports and social gatherings, and posters and postcards were among the methods adopted over the weekend to inform people

12

that they should have their gas masks fitted (7)."

Most people agreed with the Prime Minister when he spoke over the radio: "How horrible, fantastic, incredible it is that we should be digging trenches and trying on gas masks here because of a quarrel in a far away country between people of whom we know nothing (8)."

The poet, Louis MacNeice, described the dread everyone was feeling (9):

> The heavy panic that cramps the lungs and presses
> The collar down the spine.
> And when we go out into Piccadilly Circus
> They are selling and buying the late
> Special editions snatched and read abruptly
> Beneath the electric signs as crude as Fate.
> Today they were building in Oxford Street, the mortar
> Pleasant to smell.
> But it now seems futility, imbecility,
> To be building shops when nobody can tell
> What will happen next.

So when Chamberlain returned from Munich and his second meeting with Hitler saying, "I believe it is peace in our time," he was greeted with jubilation. A visitor to London that day said, "It had been like going to the funeral of everybody's wife . . . the streets and buses were silent as churches. Business had stopped and a pall of gloom which was almost a visible thing hung over the town. And then, just after lunch, he came out of an office building and saw someone laughing in the street. After that the good news spread before his eyes as he walked along (10)." *'Peace in our time'*

Appeasement was condoned in Parliament: no Conservatives voted against Chamberlain; only thirty abstained. Most people and most of the press agreed with the *Times*: "Here it is enough to praise God that he has crowned with success the efforts of good will, thereby saving the world from the illimitable catastrophe of war (11)."

The British government's provision of trenches and gas masks after the Godesberg crisis showed the type of war expected. Undoubtedly, the main attack would come from the air and it would come swiftly. The experts exaggerated German rearmament generally, and the number of her planes in particular. They also assumed that every plane would be used for bombing and that each *Fears of air attack*

13

bomb would drop accurately on its target. An Air Staff report, written after the First World War, thought it "fair to assume that in densely populated areas, such as London, there will be fifty casualties per ton of bombs dropped. Of these casualties one third will be killed and two thirds wounded (12)."

This figure, or multiplier, of fifty was derived from one fierce Zeppelin raid on London, and the German bombing of Guernica during the Spanish Civil War. The figure was accepted by the defence expert who believed that Britain must "reckon with the possibility of an air offensive against London in which six hundred tons might be dropped in a day and continued for some time . . . Nearly a quarter of a million casualties might be anticipated in the first week of a new war (13)."

To make room for these expected casualties, hospitals were told to release patients, "not on a peacetime standard of fitness, but on the assumption that only those should be retained for whom institutional treatment is necessary (14)." Nearly 140,000 patients were sent home.

Gas warfare   Gas attacks were feared just as much as devastation by bombing. People had not forgotten how soldiers in the First World War trenches had suffered from gas. Their tales had become exaggerated, adding terror to any talk about the dreaded war: "You get gas before you know, or you can realize," one civilian tells another in Henry Green's contemporary novel. "When I was out in France I have met lines of men coming back in single file, their hands on each other's shoulders, blinded (15)." The Italians had also used the weapon against the Abyssinians in 1935.

Since then it was assumed that gas would play a part in any future war. A handbook on its effects was distributed throughout the country. After reading it, Margery Allingham, the novelist, was horrified: "Ten minutes made it clear there was a lot to be learnt . . . The effects of the different stuffs were varied and sensational. Phosgene filled your lungs with water and produced gangrene of the extremities. Mustard had scarcely any odour but blinded you and ate your flesh away (16)."

Gas masks   Thirty-eight million gas masks were issued by the government
for all   in the weeks following Munich. The press was full of exhortations to the tardy to collect one from their local centre, and of photographs of the wise being fitted. This was often an unpleasant experience. One man described how he "was horribly sick after half a

14

minute, through the smell of the rubber, and have been feeling nauseated since. Two colleagues were fitting masks and had a dreadful morning with toddlers crying and screaming . . . Elderly folk looked ill, and expectant mothers fainted (17)."

The gas masks were distributed by Air Raid Precautions wardens, who also lectured in village halls and arranged air raid exercises. In 1937 local authorities had been ordered by the Home Office to take air raid precautions. During the crisis there was a call for A.R.P. volunteers. Many of them found the A.R.P. ill-organized and in-efficient. One complained: "I don't know what I should have to do in the event of an emergency. I have no definite instructions. I can't discover which section I happen to be, or who is the head warden (18)."

In November, 1938, Sir John Anderson was made Lord Privy Seal, specially responsible for A.R.P. and Civil Defence. He pushed up government expenditure for these services from £9½ millions in 1938 to £51 millions in 1939. In July, King George VI watched twenty thousand members of the Civil Defence forces march past. He described the march on the radio as "this demon-stration of the spirit of service which is everywhere present in the nation today (19)."

Rumours of the threatened war were everywhere, for example on posters that insisted on the wearing of gas masks, and in the in-formation pamphlets pushed through every letter box. "The object of this leaflet," began the first of these, "is to tell you now some of the things you ought to know if you are to be ready for the emer-gency of war. This does not mean that war is expected now, but it is everyone's duty to be prepared for the possibility of war (20)."

In March, 1939, the Germans violated the Munich Agreement by *Germans* invading Prague, the capital of Czechoslovakia. On 22nd August *invade Prague* the announcement of the Nazi-Soviet pact shattered the belief that Germany would be deterred from war by the fear of fighting on two fronts. Neville Chamberlain told King George VI: "When Parliament meets tomorrow it is our intention to ask for the passage into law during the day of the Emergency Powers Defence Bill. The Bill will not itself authorize action but will enable regulations to be made, if the need arises, under which action necessary for the defence of the country can be taken (21)." Mass Observation interviewers again questioned the public. A greengrocer an-nounced: "I haven't prepared anything. There will be no war (22)."

15

On 31st August only eighteen per cent of those surveyed expected a war.

Germans invade Poland

The following day, 1st September, 1939, German troops marched into Poland. The House of Commons were horrified that evening when Chamberlain seemed no readier to help the Poles than he had the Czechs. Winston Churchill described the scene: "When Mr. Greenwood rose to speak on behalf of the Labour Opposition, Mr. Amery from the Conservative benches cried out to him, 'Speak for England, Arthur!' This was received with loud cheers. There was no doubt that the temper of the House was for war (23)." The Cabinet insisted that an ultimatum should be sent to Hitler. It expired at eleven o'clock on Sunday, 3rd September, 1939.

At a quarter past eleven Chamberlain announced over the radio that the country was at war: "I am speaking to you from the Cabinet Room at 10, Downing Street. This morning the British Ambassador in Berlin handed the German government a final note, stating that unless we heard from them by 11 o'clock that they were prepared at once to withdraw their troops from Poland, a state of war would exist between us. I have to tell you now that no such undertaking has been received, and that consequently this country is at war with Germany (24)."

In 1939 everyone had gas masks, including the newsvendors on the street corners

2 The Phoney War 1939-40

"ALMOST AT 11.20 a.m., just as the Prime Minister had ceased talking, the air raid warning went and I seized my helmet and gas mask and went over to the strong-room at the War Office, our place of refuge. Here I found the whole War Office crowding downstairs . . . when I got over to the Horse Guards my servant told me that the whole raid had been a trial one (25)." General Ironside and thousands of others rushed into makeshift shelters at this first wail of the siren. The second one did not sound for a long time. German bombers were busy over Poland; Hitler had no wish to take on Britain at the same time. Chamberlain's War Cabinet was equally reluctant to begin hostilities. One hundred and six French divisions faced twenty-three German divisions during the Polish campaign, but no offensive was launched.

Panic

During this time nothing happened in the air or on land. Cecil Beaton, the society photographer, wrote in his diary: "The catastrophe we braced ourselves to face did not happen. A quiet stalemate was achieved on the Western front and the undramatic weeks of waiting were perhaps the dreariest of all our lives – a numbing continuation of anxiety and boredom (26)."

Neville Chamberlain believed the war could be won by blockading and starving Germany. The vital battle in the first week was at sea. The U-boats caused grave damage. Britain's greatest humiliation occurred when one actually penetrated the Orkneys naval harbour at Scapa Flow, and sank the battleship *Royal Oak* on 14th October. The public were horrified. An observer reported that, "More people than usual bought the mid-day papers, and there were several little groups on the corners, discussing the tragedy. Out of twenty-six overheard scraps of conversation picked up while wandering round

War at sea

17

the market, nineteen concerned the *Royal Oak* (27)." Britain's destruction of the German battleship, *Graf Spee*, two months later was some compensation. But these naval incidents merely punctuated what was now called the "bore war," and later by Americans, the "phoney war."

Volunteers   A million and a half men and women had enrolled in the A.R.P. services by September, 1939. Four hundred thousand of them were full time members, the rest were volunteers. All were mobilized at the outbreak of war and all had little to do. One volunteer "had joined the First Aid Nursing Yeomanry, which supplied drivers of army vehicles . . . I was recalled to sit about in a variety of F.A.N.Y. common rooms all over the country, kicking my heels . . . Days would pass before your turn came round to drive, or even maintain, an unconverted furniture van or borrowed limousine (28)." Henry Green's fictional auxiliary firemen led a quiet life: "There were still no raids and they waited at the sub-station, in their periods of duty, day and night, night and day . . . But they thought the strain of waiting for raids prodigious (29)."

Civil defence   Meanwhile, Civil Defence plans for safeguarding civilians were put into action. Precautions against the expected bombs and fires changed the appearance of London and other cities. Barrage balloons, designed to prevent low flying aircraft, introduced a novel skyscape. A diarist described them as "poised over our cities and docks and industrial centres, shining silver in the sun, or turning pink or golden or shades of blue . . . their cable singing some kind of a tune in a high wind, and just occasionally the balloon itself, lashing about with the fury of a wounded whale (30)."

Down on the ground the American journalist Ed Murrow described to his listeners at home the "piles of sand waiting to be shovelled into bags . . . Signs reading 'House to let;' those expensive shops in Bond Street all sandbagged; the windows boarded up; others criss-crossed with strips of brown paper to prevent shattering (31)." Trenches and sandbags altered country gardens as well as city streets. In Joyce Cary's fictitious Cotswold village, "Two A.R.P. men . . . arrive with picks and spades and dig an enormous trench across lawn and rose-beds, then go away to fetch timber for rivetting, and sandbags (32)."

Blackout   At night, the cities seemed even more strange. Street lighting was extinguished on 1st September, 1939, and drivers were forbidden to switch on their headlights. John Lehmann, the writer, "floundered about in the unaccustomed darkness ... bumping into patrolling wardens or huddled strangers, hailing taxis that crept along learning their new element, admiring the gigantic criss-crossing arms of the searchlights as they lit up the sudden silver bellies of the far balloons or scurrying clouds on windy nights, and found new beauty in the fall of moonlight on pavements ... torches, cigarette-lighters, flashed their momentary, tiny illuminations (33)."

Pillar box tops were painted yellow with a gas detector liquid. People, too, looked different, with their gas mask holders slung on their shoulders altering the shape of their silhouettes. A. P. Herbert, in the *Sunday Graphic*, caught the general tone of weary anticipation (34):

> *The Spring is coming. Therefore dust*
> *Your respirator while you may.*
> *The Spring is coming; and you must*
> *Be ready for the mustard spray.*
>
> *The Spring is coming. Therefore fill*
> *A bag or two with sand or clay,*
> *And pile them anywhere you will*
> *Provided they are in the way.*

"This was February, 1940," wrote Evelyn Waugh, "in that strangely cosy interlude between peace and war, when there was leave every weekend and plenty to eat and drink and smoke, when France stood firm on the Maginot Line and the Finns stood firm in Finland and everyone said what a cruel Winter they must be having in Germany (35)."

The soldiers with leave every weekend were mainly conscripts. **Conscripts** In the May before the outbreak of war, Chamberlain had introduced the idea of conscription against fierce opposition. Anthony Wedgwood Benn spoke for many in the Labour Party: "We want the cause put before the country. Then we shall get the men. I do feel very deeply that this Bill is an insult to this country. We believe that if you give the people an ideal to fight for they will fight (36)."

Only young men of twenty and twenty-one years' old were affected by the Bill, and were called up with the regulars on 31st August. Ed Murrow broadcast to the States: "This afternoon we learned that the Navy has been fully mobilized; all reservists have been called up for the Army, and the Royal Air Force has called up part of its reserves. They are being called up by radio. There's none

Left During the blackout, motor vehicles were not allowed to use lights.
Right Searchlights pierce the night sky to locate enemy aircraft

of the usual business of individual notices (37)."

On 3rd September, 1939, the National Service Act brought in all men between eighteen and forty-one years' old, except for those engaged in reserved occupations. It was June, 1941, before the Act caught up with the forty year olds. While conscription was slow, the mobilization of regulars was not too efficient. Evelyn Waugh's hero "was in uniform, acutely uncomfortable in ten-year-old trousers. He had been to report at the headquarters and was home . . . collecting his kit which, in the two years since he was last at camp had been misused in charades and picnics and dispersed about the house in a dozen improbable places. His pistol, in particular, had been a trouble . . . At length the nursery-maid found it at the back of the toy cupboard (38)."

In January, 1940, the press attacked the extended call-up of six more age groups: "Britain is to possess by the end of this year an army of $3\frac{1}{2}$ million men. We are to prepare on the assumption that huge land battles will provide the main feature of this war. In fact, there is every indication that gruelling warfare in the seas together with superior industrial stamina may settle the issue (39)." Op-

This coffee shop is heavily sandbagged against possible bomb damage. But it was "Business as usual."

timists and pessimists alike envisaged a short war with little ground fighting. A Member of Parliament wrote to his wife: "It will either be all over in August, or else we shall have won. Hitler will not be able to go on into next year (40)."

Women volunteers increased the ranks of the forces. An American visitor explained that "W.A.A.F. means Women's Auxiliary Air Force. A Waaf is a young lady in active military service. Collectively she is the secretariat of the Air Force. All the Air Force officers I talked to about the Waafs were very enthusiastic about them, said they were hard working, efficient, professional (41)." The Wrens, the Women's Royal Naval Service, enticed many girls with its smart uniform and promises of foreign travel. The novelist, Pamela Frankau, wrote of her experiences in the A.T.S. (Auxiliary Territorial Service) in a women's magazine: "Here I go again, out of step, and my arms want to swing in the same way as my legs . . . I've done House Orderly and Naafi and Bath House but they say that Recruits Pantry is the worst (42)." Conscription for unmarried women between twenty and thirty was introduced in December, 1941.

Women volunteers

21

Few conscripts refused their call-up papers. Six in every thousand registered as conscientious objectors, but they were allowed to take approved work in industry or agriculture, or as non-combatants in the forces. Some pressure was put on young men to join up. Kingsley Martin, the Editor of the *New Statesman* described how "a brass hat in a first class carriage, which also held a young man in civilian clothes, made a point of speaking somewhat more loudly than was necessary to his neighbour about young men who ought to be in uniform (43)."

But there was no strong feeling against the C.O.'s. A diarist described how "a young undergraduate came in to dinner. The last time we had seen him he had told us that he was an intellectual pacifist and was going to register as a conscientious objector. Now he has done so and is shortly beginning work with the Quakers. In the war of 1914-18 a conscientious objector was voted a coward. Today we are better able to grasp that the highly educated theorist can so look at war that he can convince himself that it is the most evil thing on earth (44)."

In any case, pacifism was not strong. Times had changed since the Oxford Union's resolution in 1933 when it would "under no circumstances fight for its King and Country." Fenner Brockway, a sincere pacifist of the thirties, "was too conscious of the evil of Nazism and Fascism to be completely pacifist (45)."

Meanwhile, conscripts and regulars were called to recruiting centres and unit headquarters. They were then dispatched to training centres and scattered camps. Roads and railways were full of uniformed figures. In the first few days of the war the whole country seemed to be on the move. Evelyn Waugh wrote: "Everywhere houses were being closed, furniture stored, children transported . . . everywhere little groups of friends were arranging to spend the war together (46)." Cars poured out of London. Whole departments of Civil Servants took over resort hotels. The Bank of England transferred itself to a Hampshire village, Billingsgate fish market was dispersed to various centres. Five thousand prisoners and borstal boys were given their freedom.

The biggest movement of all, however, was that of the evacuees. After Munich, Sir John Anderson had devised a scheme to evacuate people from the cities which might be bombed. The country was divided into evacuation, neutral, and reception areas. On 1st September, a newspaper reported that "the evacuation of three

Facing page Women like these "Wrens" (Women's Royal Naval Service) played a full part in the armed services

million children, mothers, hospital patients and blind people from congested areas to safety zones throughout Britain began at 5.30 a.m. today. Their transport will involve many changes in railway timetables, and certain roads out of London will be closed to inward traffic (47)." Posters—showing forlorn children—begged: "Mothers, send them out of London!" Only one and a half million took advantage of the government's plans for transport and billets. Two million others independently joined the exodus.

Secret destinations A London schoolgirl described her week before the outbreak of war: "We were told that the order to evacuate might come through at any moment . . . So all that week we came to school in the morning, after fond farewells and the hurried making of sandwiches, and all that week we returned home in the evening and ate our sandwiches for supper . . . On Thursday the uncertainty was ended . . . We marched in twos, heartily cheered on our way by the inhabitants of Camden Town. We stood on the station platform feeling rather subdued. At last the train came and we bundled in. Only the engine driver knew our destination (48)." For other children, the experience was more traumatic. Bernard Kops and his school friends "assembled in the playground with our gas masks and labels tied to our coats. And then we all moved away, all the children and all the parents crying (49)."

On the long journeys in the trains without corridors many children wet themselves, wept for their mothers, became very dirty and hungry. Often when they arrived "no organization existed for dealing with them. Schools and other buildings were opened, but bedding and blankets did not exist. In some cases for four days they lived—mothers, teachers and children—on an official diet of milk, apples and cheese, sleeping on straw covered by grain bags (50)."

By the time their billets were arranged they did not appear very attractive guests. An observer in a Liverpool reception area reported: "The state of the children was such that the school had to be fumigated after the reception. Except for a small number, the children were filthy and we have never seen so many verminous children lacking any knowledge of clean and hygienic habits . . . Clothing was dirty and footgear inadequate, the majority wearing old plimsolls (51)."

24 *Social surprises* Many of the children came from slum conditions quite unknown to country people. Ninety per cent of those from Stepney (London),

sixty-six per cent from York, and eighty per cent from Glasgow, lived in houses without baths. One boy was astonished that, "Everything was so clean . . . We were even given flannels and tooth brushes. We'd never cleaned our teeth up till then. And hot water came from the tap. And there was a lavatory upstairs. And carpets. And something called an eiderdown. And clean sheets. This was all very odd. And rather scaring (52)." The children, especially from Leeds and London, were "used to fish and chips and something in their hands for dinner (53)." Hot dinners and hot baths were not the only surprises awaiting them. In the cities the seasons had been indistinguishable. One child told her mother: "They call this Spring, mum, and they have one down here every year (54)." Bernard Kops "realized that the world was an open place of light, air and clouds (55)."

Ancient social barriers were broken down as town and country people came into contact. Villagers met a completely new type of person, not only in the evacuees, but in the officials from the towns. The welfare officer posted to Margery Allingham's Essex village "was something quite new on my horizon. She turned out to be very Left wing, a little more informed about facts than people, full of complete misinformation about the country upper classes (56)." On the other hand a Member of Parliament wrote in his diary that, "Much ill feeling has been caused . . . the interesting thing is that this feeling is not between the rich and the poor, but between the urban and the rural poor (57)." Cottagers were shocked at the laziness and unhelpfulness of the city mothers, complaining that they had no wish to knit, sew or cook and that "pictures and novelettes were their one desire (58)."

The country people on the whole were extraordinarily generous in their acceptance of the thousands of evacuees. Apart from natural sympathy with the homeless children, many—like the farmer in Joyce Cary's novel—"Had the feeling that war, since it was a misfortune, ought to bring some hardships . . . They complained of the vackies for leaving gates open, breaking the ripe corn, letting the pigs into the garden, but usually they added with various tones of resignation or bitterness: 'But there, it's the war' (59)." Nor were they helped by poor remuneration. Kingsley Martin wrote about "the difficulty which working-class householders find in keeping lads on eight shillings and sixpence a week. If you have about thirty shillings a week, as the labourers have in our

Rural problems

village, after paying their insurance, you've not much left for new mattresses and so forth (60)."

The country gentry reacted less well to the evacuees than the poorer cottagers. Partly because the billeting officers were drawn from the middle classes. "The cottages of the agricultural labourers were crowded with the exhausted evacuees but the manor houses and the weekend cottages were permitted to keep their spare rooms empty, 'waiting for relatives' (61)." A diarist commented that when the middle classes did take in evacuees they "are sometimes rigidly exclusive and too much hide-bound by class distinctions to offer friendship to families with a different social background (62)."

Boredom

As the Winter of 1939 wore on the cities remained free from raids. More and more complaints came from both the bored evacuees who had not returned home, and from their harrassed hosts. All, according to a Member of Parliament speaking in the House, "appeared to think that the whole thing was quite unnecessary and merely a government game (63)." Most people felt quite divorced from the government. An official poster announcing: "*Your* courage, *your* cheerfulness, *your* resolution will bring *us* victory" was accepted without demur; it typified the attitude of both rulers and ruled. Chamberlain and his Ministers failed to understand the people's mood, fearing to antagonize them by too many regulations.

Rationing

But, as shipping casualties brought food shortages and high prices, most people expected and wanted rationing. A Lancashire housewife complained: "I wish to goodness they would introduce rationing. At least I would be able to go into a shop and get what I was allowed. As it is I've got to beg . . . this constant scrounging is getting on my nerves (64)." As one writer put it, however, "rationing, which I had imagined would be clamped down on us . . . was still a long way off (65)." The press announced in November that "rationing of food is to begin gently, quite partially and not immediately . . . There is to be another six weeks' respite before any official limitation of retail sales is enforced in respect of the two commodities—butter and bacon—which will first be rationed (66)."

The grumbling grew as the evacuees returned to their city homes. One grievance concerned the amount of taxpayers' money spent on Civil Defence. Recruits were accused of army dodging. A

26

traveller complained of the "trains which are slow, crowded and devoid of restaurants. Before nightfall the blinds are drawn down and the railway carriage, if lighted at all, is illumined by a blue pinpoint of light (67)."

Transport, prices, evacuation and food brought complaints, but worst of all was the blackout. One journalist asked: "This travelling back from work in the evening unable to read the paper—is it necessary? Does any sense lie in depressing and irritating people unduly? (68)." As well as the dreariness, there was the constant annoyance at having to black out every chink of light by black curtains, paper, blinds or wooden contraptions. If this was not done, the A.R.P. warden would soon come knocking on the door.

The blackout brought its own dangers. Between September *Life in* and November 1939, deaths from raids were nil and those from *the blackout* air raid precautions three thousand. John Lehmann wrote: "There were many accidents in the streets those first days—a man heard moaning but not seen—a tin hatted policeman running into a pub to telephone for an ambulance—it seemed fantastic not to use light on such occasions, but the discipline held everyone in its grip (69)." Road deaths increased by a hundred per cent. Everyone had their own blackout story. "They spoke of incidents and crimes in the blackout. So-and-so had lost all her teeth in a taxi. So-and-so had been sandbagged . . . So-and-so had been knocked down by an ambulance and left for dead (70)." The *Daily Herald* reported that, "Authorities in three towns have appealed for relaxation of the lighting restrictions following blackout street accidents (71)."

The intense cold, the ice and snow of that winter, intensified the inconveniences of the blackout. Impatience and dissatisfaction with the boring war further increased with the fiasco of the Finnish campaign. There was still no activity on the French-German border. When the British Secretary for Air was asked why he did not take the offensive by bombing German factories in the Black Forest, he replied: "Are you aware it is private property? Why, you will be asking me to bomb Essen next (72)."

Thus, the government was equally slow to face the realities of *"Cato"* war on the battle front and on the home front. An anti-government tract was published by three journalists under the pseudonym "Cato." It spoke for many: "The British government did not exert itself to any great extent even after we had clashed into war

with one of the most tremendous military powers of all times . . .
In order to quieten the apprehensions of the citizens, Ministers
and Generals began to make speeches calculated to encourage the
public in the belief that the war was already won (73)." Neville
Chamberlain himself was guilty on this count. In April, 1940, he
told the Conservative Party: "After seven months of war I feel
ten times as confident of victory as I did at the beginning. Whatever
it was that Hitler thought he might get away with, one thing is
certain: he missed the bus (74)."

Chamberlain departs   But a few days later Hitler "caught the bus" in Scandinavia.
His armies marched through Denmark to occupy Norway just
as the British Navy, sent by the government under pressure for
action, were mining Norwegian waters. In just a month the British
expeditionary force was back in the sea. Public opinion hardened.
The *Daily Mail* came out with a strong editorial: "The country
wants a new government composed of men of drive, initiative and
proved efficiency under new leadership . . . Mr. Chamberlain and
his Government have completely lost the confidence of the nation
(75)." An ex-minister brought the attack on Chamberlain to a
head: "We cannot go on as we are . . . The next essential is swift,
decisive action . . . This is what Cromwell said to the Long Parliament when he thought it was no longer fit to conduct the affairs of
the nation: 'You have sat too long here for any good you have been
doing. Depart, I say, and let us have done with you. In the name
of God, go' (76)."

Winston Churchill   The government's majority fell from 240 to 81. The rebels
demanded a coalition government. The Labour and Liberal Parties
refused to serve under Chamberlain, but were willing to accept
either Lord Halifax or Winston Churchill. The Prime Minister
met the two possible leaders on 9th May, 1940. Churchill, by
keeping silent, forced Halifax to admit the difficulties of a peer
leading the country at such a time. The next evening King George
VI called Churchill to Buckingham Palace and asked him to form
a government.

3 Dunkirk: The Island Fortress

WHEN WINSTON CHURCHILL retired to bed on 10th September, 1940, he was "conscious of a profound sense of relief. At last I had the authority to give directions over the whole scene. I felt as if I were walking with destiny, and that all my past life has been but a preparation for this hour and for this trial (77)." He had been out of office for ten years before the outbreak of war and was now sixty-five years' old.

Churchill's destiny

Churchill's coalition war Cabinet was small: Lord Halifax and Neville Chamberlain from the Right, Clement Attlee and Arthur Greenwood from the Left. Lord Woolton stayed at the Ministry of Food, and Sir Kingsley Wood became Chancellor of the Exchequer. Sir John Anderson took the Home Office. An opinion poll showed that, "Probably no Cabinet Minister has a lower public appeal . . . His rather formal and uncompromising manner has never infused into the machinery for which he is responsible any warmth, humour or general sympathy likely to appeal to the many (78)." Yet Anderson's sound sense and administrative ability won Churchill's confidence. He succeeded Chamberlain in the War Cabinet in October, 1940.

But Churchill did not rely entirely on Chamberlain's men. One radio listener reported: "New appointments to the Cabinet came through every few hours. One can make all sorts of criticisms, but the decisive fact seems to be that a breach has at last been made in the concrete defences of the Old Gang (79)." Lord Beaverbrook, a friend of Churchill's and the energetic proprietor of the *Daily Express*, was given the Ministry of Aircraft Production. The appointment of Ernest Bevin to the Ministry of Labour, which was soon to include National Service, was more popular.

Lord Beaverbrook

Left Winston Churchill soon after he became Prime Minister, leaving 10 Downing Street. *Right* Ernest Bevin, Churchill's Minister of Labour

Both men joined the War Cabinet in August.

Ernest Bevin   Bevin had begun his working life as a farm-hand and delivery boy. He had worked his way through the Trade Union movement to become the respected and tough boss of the Transport and General Workers Union. He was now sixty years' old and took his place in the House of Commons for the first time. The novelist, J. B. Priestley, described him on the front bench as "a powerful thick-set determined figure of a man, a fine lump of that England which we all love; one of those men who stand up among the cowardices and treacheries and corruption of this recent world like an oak tree in a swamp (80)."

Blood, toil,   The Prime Minister himself took the title of Minister of Defence.
tears and He wished to be personally responsible for the military direction
sweat of the war. He faced a desperate situation (Hitler had invaded Holland and Belgium the day he took office) with immense confidence: "I thought I knew a good deal about it, and I was sure I should not fail (81)." The suspicions of the Tory backbenchers were overcome in a few weeks. One of them described Churchill

30   as "very stout and black, smoothing his palms down across his

frame—beginning by patting his chest, then smoothing his stomach and ending down at the groin (82)." He imparted his confidence to Members of Parliament and to the whole nation, when he spoke first in the House and then over the radio: "I have nothing to offer but blood, toil, tears and sweat. You ask, What is our aim? I can answer in one word: Victory—victory at all costs (83)."

Churchill's oratory gave the war an immediate reality: at last *Invasion fears* people began to feel that this was not only the government's struggle: it was their own. The advance of the British and French into the Netherlands, and the breakthrough of the German armies into France brought the war—literally—nearer home. Invasion was now a real threat. In an Essex village "everybody came out into the streets to talk. Invasion was in the wind and the advance air attack expected every second (84)."

Harold Nicolson, Parliamentary Secretary at the Ministry of Information, wrote to his wife in Kent. "I don't think that even if the Germans occupied Sissinghurst they would harm you. But to be quite sure that you are not put to any humiliation I think you really ought to have a 'bare bodkin' handy so that you can take your quietus when necessary. I shall have one also (85)." He went "down to the War Office to discuss [with an official] the question of civilian morale in case of invasion. He [the official] feels pretty certain that the Germans will attempt to make an attack on London, and he says that the possibility of evacuating the Channel and East Coast towns is now being considered (86)." Mothers and children who had been taken out of London to East Anglia, Kent and Sussex were now sent on to South Wales and the West country. Between May and July 200,000 more children left the cities in a second wave of evacuation.

The French were unable to hold back the invaders. On 20th May, *Dunkirk* 1940, the Germans reached the Channel coast. The British Expeditionary Force was cut off in the country behind Dunkirk. Churchill was forced to agree that another offensive was impossible, and evacuation the only alternative. This in itself was a frightening task. How could 400,000 men be taken off the beaches and shipped home? A government broadcast appealed for all sea-worthy boats to brave enemy mines and make the terrifying journey. Eight hundred and sixty ships took part in Operation "Dynamo." They included fishing boats and holiday steamers. As J. B. Priestley said: "We've known them and laughed at them, these fussy little

31

steamers, all our lives . . . Sometimes they only went as far as the next seaside resort. They seemed to belong to the same ridiculous holiday world as pierrots and piers . . . But they were called out of that world . . . Yes, these *Brighton Belles* and *Brighton Queens* left that innocent foolish world of theirs to sail into the inferno, to defy bombs, shells, magnetic mines, torpedoes, machine-gun fire— to rescue our soldiers (87)."

Harold Nicolson went down to the coast: "We have now evacuated 220,000 men which is amazing when I recall how we feared we should lose eighty per cent . . . We pass twelve trains packed with tired dirty but cheering troops (88)." By the end of the operation 338,226 men were rescued. There was jubilation. But Churchill looked ahead: "We shall go on to the end, we shall fight in France, we shall fight in the seas and oceans, we shall fight with growing confidence and growing strength in the air, we shall defend our island, whatever the cost may be; we shall fight on the beaches, we shall fight on the landing grounds, we shall fight in the fields and in the streets, we shall fight in the hills (89)."

The Germans turned south instead of crossing the Channel. Mussolini, seeing the plight of France, thought this would be a good time to join Hitler and declare war on the allies. The French capitulated on 17th June, 1940. Churchill told the House of Commons that, "What General Weygand called the Battle of France is over. I expect the Battle of Britain is about to begin . . . Let us therefore brace ourselves to our duties and so bear ourselves that, if the British Empire and its Commonwealth last for a thousand years, men will still say, 'This was their finest hour' (90)."

Britain at bay   Britain now stood alone facing a German-occupied Europe. The Channel no longer gave her the same defence as in the days before bomber aircraft. Her shipping and imports were imperilled by enemy control of the Mediterranean, as well as by mines and U-boats. Nevertheless, there was some feeling of relief that matters had been brought to a head. King George VI wrote to his mother: "Personally I feel happier now that we have no allies to be polite to and pamper (91)." One editor commented on the absence of any general panic. He was "astounded once again at the imperturbability of the British people. I no longer think that they are unmoved because they are unawakened: it is mainly that a sense of British invincibility has always been part of their make-up; and the man-in-the-street is determined to carry on with his

British troops were driven out of Europe by the Germans. They evacuated from Dunkirk on the north coast of France.

allotment or his bicycling club as long as possible. It is his way of showing that Hitler can't get him down (92)."

The government, however, feared a general panic if ever German forces should actually land. An official notice appeared in the press appealing to everyone to remain calm: "I do not get panicky. I stay put. I do not say, 'I must get out of here.' I remember that fighting men must have clear roads. I do not go on to the road on bicycle, in a car or on foot. Whether I am at work or at home, I just stay put (93)."

George Orwell wanted the government to arm civilians against *Home guard* the expected invaders: "There is talk of arming some of the Local Defence Volunteer contingents with shotguns . . . the distribution should be made now (94)." He also described to his readers how the L.D.V., which was later known as the Home Guard, was raised: "in response to a radio appeal by Anthony Eden, following on the success of the German parachute troops in Holland. It got a quarter of a million troops in the first twenty-four hours (95)." Response from part-time unpaid volunteers was enthusiastic all over the country. J. B. Priestley said that in his village they "represented a good cross section of English rural life; we had a parson, a bailiff, a builder, farmers and farm labourers (96)." In a London headquarters a diarist reported, "a mixed bunch. We have amongst others, a Polish company director, two electrical engineers, a student, the sales manager of Dunlop's, [and] a youth employed at Carreras . . . (97)."

The Home Guard engaged in apparently schoolboy exercises. One volunteer "went out in a car to do a reconnaissance of the approaches to Euston Station which we are to attempt to capture tomorrow in a Home Guard exercise. Worked out an ingenious route which may prove successful (98)." But by 1941 they could, in Orwell's words, "be regarded as a serious force, capable of strong resistance for at any rate a short period . . . The Home Guard relieves the army of some of its routine patrols, pickets on buildings and does a certain amount of A.R.P. work (99)."

Invasion precautions
Everywhere there was evidence of the fear of invasion. Signposts were blacked out, on government orders, so that the invaders would lose their way. In reality, only English motorists were confused by this action. The southern resorts were transformed. Troops, like Evelyn Waugh's fictitious battalion, "lined the sands with barbed wire and demolished the steps leading from esplanade to beach; they dug weapon pits in the corporation's gardens, sandbagged the bow-windows of private houses and blocked the roads with dragon's teeth and pill boxes (100)." When J. B. Priestley visited the seaside town of Margate he "wandered round, and sometimes through large empty hotels. The few signs of life only made the whole place seem more unreal and spectral (101)."

Dunkirk spirit
In any case, there was little time for vacations. Ernest Bevin said: "The people have cheerfully abandoned their holidays, and are taking to new methods for exercise. Grounds that were used for football have been taken over for physical training, and thousands of arms workers, Civil Defence units and men waiting for call up are taking full advantage of the opportunities offered (102)." Lord Beaverbrook's call for longer working hours and increased production aroused enthusiastic public support—the famous "Dunkirk spirit." Factories were open twenty-four hours, seven days a week. Most people worked from 8 a.m. until 7 p.m. Bank holidays were ignored.

The frightened government gave the Home Secretary the right, under an extended Defence Regulation 18b, to imprison without

Everyone feared an invasion. Signposts were torn up to confuse the enemy

trial anyone he believed to endanger the safety of the realm. A leader writer commented: "This is a Discipline Act and it will be eagerly accepted (103)." The Fascist party was the first victim. The press announced: "Sir Oswald Mosley and eight members of his Fascist organization were arrested by Scotland Yard men (104)."

Refugees and all "enemy aliens" were especially vulnerable *Enemy aliens* under Regulation 18b. By the beginning of the war there were already 60,000 German and Austrian refugees in Britain, and 8,000 Czechs, soon to be joined by Belgians and Dutch, including Queen Wilhelmina of the Netherlands. Bishop Bell, the humane bishop of Chichester, believed "that it is possible to absorb in this country a far greater number of refugees than have yet been envisaged (105)." But not many shared his liberal attitude. The works manager in J. B. Priestley's novel, *Black-out in Gretley*,

35

complained of the German refugees roaming about the town until we don't know where we are (106)." This reaction was far more typical.

When war was declared, every alien in the country had to appear before a tribunal. Most were left alone, some were not allowed to travel, and a minority were actually interned. This minority swelled to 2,000 from the south coast alone after the scare of Hitler's invasion of Belgium and Holland. Feelings ran high. The slogan "Intern the lot," was scrawled on walls. The *Daily Mail* urged "a far stricter supervision of all aliens (107)." Ed Murrow told his American listeners that, "Refugees arriving from the Continent are being closely questioned in an effort to weed out spies (108)."

Internees

Unlucky and innocent aliens were snatched away from their homes and families, much as German Jews were marched off to concentration camps. But their subsequent fate, though it included damp rat-infested Lancashire Mills on the way to Isle of Man camps, was not so ghastly. But it was bad enough for a Member of Parliament to say: "I shall not feel happy, either as an English-man or a supporter of the government, until this bespattered page of our history has been cleared up, and rewritten (109)."

A year later only four hundred remained in custody, including Sir Oswald Mosley and his wife. The rest often had trouble finding work; but they were free within limits, although frequently subject to curfew and other restrictions. When a reporter visited Anna Freud, the psychiatrist daughter of Sigmund, "She told me the only thing she missed in the war was her radio. I asked her where it was. She said, 'They took it away because I am an alien' (110)." Her interviewer was himself an alien and therefore had to register with the police like all others, telling the "particulars of my passport, where I intended to live, what I intended to do and where I intended to go (111)."

Aliens were suspected as potential collaborators in the event of invasion. The *Daily Mail* believed that "Holland fell in five days because no one could trust his neighbour. This must not happen in Britain (112)." It had already happened in the Channel Islands, occupied by the Germans in June, 1940. Claud Cockburn remonstrated about the quislings—the name borrowed from the Norwegian collaborator, Quisling. But he was told, "You don't understand, Claud old boy ... at the time they did that, those people thought the Germans were going to win (113)."

Quislings

37

Facing page. Top Winston Churchill sees for himself a gun emplacement on the south coast of England. *Bottom* Members of the Home Guard prepare against invasion in their quiet village

Future quislings might already be spying. Suspicions were exacerbated by "Cooper's Snoopers," men appointed by Duff Cooper to encourage neighbours to inform on each other. But Churchill put an end to their demoralising activity. Tommy Handley's B.B.C. comedy programme—*It's That Man Again*—introduced a character called Funf, the very image of the feared spy. In an Essex village "fifth column excitement was mounting to fever pitch (114)." It often reached absurd limits. Evelyn Waugh's intelligence officer told Guy Crouchback: "Fifth columnists will be your special concern . . . Suspect everyone—the vicar, the village grocer, the farmer whose family have lived there a hundred years, all the most unlikely people (115)." Fact was no more absurd than fiction. When the producer Humphrey Jennings was making his feature film about life in the Auxiliary Fire Service, *Fires were Started*, his actors were unrecognized by the real firemen, and were accused of being fifth columnists.

German radio propaganda cleverly exaggerated the growing suspicions. A *Daily Express* journalist writing about enemy broadcasts commented: "A gent I'd like to meet is moaning periodically from Zeeson. He speaks English of the haw-haw, damit-get-out-of-my-way variety (116)." This was William Joyce, an American born Mosleyite who had decided to leave London for Berlin and had taken a job in broadcasting when he could find no other work. Joyce was thus re-christened "Lord Haw-Haw." Cassandra in the *Daily Mirror* treated him as a good joke: "I earnestly ask all of you who are able to listen . . . to do so (117)." But another journalist warned his readers: "Historians of this country may well have something to say about the mistake that has been made, by reason of extravagant publicity for this dreary

name, in directing national attention to the potentially dangerous system of enemy propaganda against this country's morale (118)."

Careless talk costs lives

Six million people listened regularly to these propaganda broadcasts, and eighteen million occasionally to Lord Haw-Haw. They talked among themselves, exaggerating his threats. Production in a Midlands' factory dropped after rumours that he had forecast a local air raid. Kingsley Martin wrote in June, 1940: "We know now that no such threats have ever come from Haw-Haw, and all the stories about his uncanny knowledge of places . . . are untrue (119)." Official posters warned the rumour mongers that "Careless talk costs lives." A. P. Herbert begged his readers (120):

> Do not believe the tale the milkman tells;
> No troops have mutinied at Potters Bar.
> Nor are there submarines at Tunbridge Wells.
> The B.B.C. will warn us when there are.

Postscripts series

In March, 1940, the B.B.C. launched its *Postscripts* series in answer to Haw-Haw. Every Sunday evening J. B. Priestley boosted the courage of the ordinary Englishman against the Fascists: "Let the Nazis in, and you will find that the laziest loud-mouth in the workshop has suddenly been given power to kick you up and down the street (121)." A political note was soon heard in his broadcasts: "Property is that old-fashioned way of thinking of a country as a thing, and a collection of things . . . all owned by certain people, instead of thinking of a country as the home of a living society. Near where I live is a house with a large garden that's not being used at all because the owner of it has gone to America. There are hundreds of working men not far from here who urgently need ground for allotments so that they can produce a bit more food. Also, we may soon need more houses for billeting. Therefore, I say, that house and garden ought to be used whether the owner who's gone to America likes it or not (122)."

Class differences

The government did not like such preaching. George Orwell wrote in his diary that "Priestley, whose Sunday night broadcasts were by implication socialist propaganda, has been shoved off the air, evidently at the insistence of the Conservative Party (123)."

In spite of the B.B.C., socialist ideas gained ground as class resentment increased. Even a *Times* correspondent wrote indignantly that the people who grumbled most about the effects of the war "seem to be the ones who have nothing more precious to lose than a

39

Facing page Surrounded by barbed wire, this seaside tea house serves as a military strongpoint sense of material security and a comfortable certainty that while they are down at dinner, a well-trained housemaid will go into the drawing-room and plump up the cushions (124)."

It was easier for the rich than the poor to avoid the unpleasantness of war. A visitor to the Dorchester Hotel in London found "the valeting and the lady's maiding as conscientious and as smoothly self-effacing as ever (125)." There were even luxury gas mask containers to point class differences in the streets. Priestley had been scornful of the English rich who escaped to America: "thousands of wealthy men and women whose sole aim was to get as much money as possible from this country to America . . . Many started exporting their commodities as fast as possible, following them with their wives, their showgirls and, finally, themselves (126)."

Funkholes   Other people escaped to safe areas without going abroad. Country hotels suddenly did a roaring trade. They were nick-named "funkholes." Looking for a room for the night in the West Country, Priestley met laughter and hints "that they had been full for weeks and would remain full for months. I said there appeared to be a surprising number of people travelling in these rather out-of-the-way parts and was told that all these guests weren't travellers but resident guests; people who had settled in these hotels to be out of the way of sirens and anti-aircraft guns and bombs (127)." Hotel advertisements appeared in the press offering, in Exmouth, "comfort and cuisine in a safe area (128)."

New attitudes   Class resentments, and the fear of invasion, both made people think about the future and the structure of their society. A traveller was told by a local man that, "Many Jarrow people would like to see done much of the levelling up that Hitler has done, but not in the Hitler fashion (129)." Orwell put the extreme view: "I doubt whether many people under fifty believe . . . that England can win the war without passing through revolution (130)."

The *Times* did not advocate Orwell's idea of revolution. But in July, 1940, it did come out with a remarkable editorial: "If we speak of democracy, we do not mean a democracy which maintains the right to vote, but forgets the right to work and the right to live. If we speak of freedom, we do not mean a rugged individualism which excludes social organization and economic planning. If we speak of equality, we do not mean a political equality nullified by social and economic privilege (131)." The first bombs had not yet fallen; but the war was already changing many long held attitudes.

4 The Blitz of 1940

FRANCE FELL on the 17th June, 1940. But the expected attack on Britain did not follow at once. Hitler still hoped to negotiate a peace settlement. Churchill and his Cabinet never considered the possibility; they used the unlooked for respite to improve Britain's defences. Estimates of German bombing capabilities were exaggerated, and this—coupled with the fact that Beaverbrook was Minister of Aircraft Production—led the main effort being put into the provision of fighter planes: 446 left the factories in June, and 496 in July, as opposed to 256 in April.

The public were as determined as the government to fight Hitler. *Public mood* They felt the war to be their own and were prepared to make the financial sacrifices asked of them. Kingsley Wood's April budget, though orthodox, introduced Purchase Tax for the first time. One writer made an entry in her diary: "Now for the pain in the neck budget. It's tough. Postage $2\frac{1}{2}$d., Postcards up to 2d. Super tax from £1,500 a year. Still, it's worth it if it stops Hitler (132)." The increased taxes on beer and tobacco aroused grumbles but no greater objections. A. P. Herbert's comment was as mild as the general reaction (133):

> *From vile tobacco, brandy, beer*
> *From whisky, wine and gin*
> *Three hundred million pounds a year*
> *The Chancellor draws in.*
> *And it is terrible to think*
> *What hangs on you and me;*
> *For if we did not smoke or drink*
> *Where would our country be?*

Beaverbrook involved everyone, not only the factory workers, *Fighter planes* in his fanatical drive for fighter planes. He appealed: "Women of Britain, give us your aluminium. We want it and we want it now . . . The need is instant. The call is urgent. Our expectations are high. We will turn your pots and pans into Spitfires, Hurricanes, Blenheims and Wellingtons (134)." The response was enthusiastic. Women emptied their kitchens of saucepans as readily as everyone gave up the railings around their gardens in reply to a government order. Eighteen months later a Member of Parliament reported that "Over 370,000 tons of railings have been gathered as a result of the policy pursued throughout the country. That is a very powerful contribution to the scrap required (135)."

Spitfires and Hurricanes

Money was donated to the Spitfire and Hurricane funds set up in many towns and villages. One "elderly woman went to the suburban office of a London Spitfire fund, emptied her bag full of shillings, said 'For years I've been saving these to divorce my husband, but Hitler is far more wicked. You'd better have the money' (136)." A journalist reported that, "Every form of tie which can be said to unite people is at this moment being very properly exploited to charm money out of their pockets for worthy objects. Among such links is the common property in a Christian name. The Margarets of the Empire have just handed over the first of several mobile canteens and the Doreens are proposing to buy a Spitfire (137)."

In fact, the production of fighters was limited more by lack of factory capacity than lack of money. Moreover, the Air Force was even more short of men than of planes. Over half the pilots were volunteers in need of training. It was to save their strength that Air Marshal "Stuffy" Dowding refused to use all his planes against the German attacks on British convoys through the Straits of Dover, which began in earnest on 10th July, 1940.

Operation Sealion

Hitler now ordered plans for Operation "Sealion," the invasion of England. But he still hankered after a negotiated peace. At the beginning of August, people in southern England awoke to find their gardens littered with leaflets advocating a settlement. "Hitler has found a new weapon—the leaflet. His airmen dropped thousands of them . . . It has four pages, is the size of a small newspaper . . . It contains Hitler's speech, 'A last appeal to Reason' (138)." The *Daily Mirror* printed its report under a huge photograph of four women laughing aloud as they read the pamphlet. There were never any real grounds for the fear that the people would demand negotiations for peace. The government's careful silence

42

The dread of war: Two German Dornier bombers fly over London by the River Thames

on the arrival of Rudolf Hess in Scotland in May, 1941, in case he might rally support for such a demand, was quite unnecessary.

German attacks on British convoys gave way to the bombing of airfields. Hermann Goering ordered the *Luftwaffe* (airforce) to destroy the R.A.F. by bombing the Kent fighter bases. The Battle of Britain had begun. The press reported that on one night, "More than six hundred German planes were used in three raids on South East England . . . Twice the raiders were beaten . . . During the second raid there were terrific combats over the Thames (139)." The radar system (see Chapter 7) helped the fighters intercept and bring down the bombers. Luckily, only the stations at Ventnor and Dover were bombed.

Battle of Britain

The Germans underestimated the importance of these stations in providing an early warning system. By the middle of August they had lost 236 planes at a cost of 95 to the British. The success of the fighter pilots was due partly to radar and partly to their own extraordinary bravery. One hundred and three more people were killed, and one hundred and twenty-eight wounded during the next three weeks. The remaining few became utterly exhausted on their

43

nerve racked flights. One of them wrote: "We were dead. We were too tired even to get drunk (140)."

Just as the pilots were nearing the end of their strength the Germans switched their effort from the airfields to London. Partly they were in a hurry to beat the coming of Autumn, and partly they intended a reprisal against the British bombing of Berlin on 25th August. On 7th September a visitor watched as "the white puffballs of anti-aircraft fire began to appear against a steel blue sky. The first flight of German bombers were coming up the river (141)."

On the river itself, in a Thames Auxiliary patrol boat, A. P. Herbert saw the raid: "Every reach was bright with the conflagrations. Bombers were roaring and bumbling overhead and as we passed a bomb whistled over Parliament into Westminster. We rounded Limehouse Corner and saw a stupendous spectacle. Half a mile or more of Surrey shore was burning, the mountains of precious timber in the docks, bankside wharves and warehouses, two piers and wooden barges. The wind was westerly, and the accumulated smoke and sparks of all the fires swept in a high wall right across the river (142)."

A journalist told his American readers, "Hitler almost took London in an almost continuous succession of mass raids which had the city ringed in fire (143)." In one day the Germans lost in one raid 185 planes and the British 60. The *Luftwaffe's* effort to knock out the R.A.F. and secure a safe sea passage for the invaders had failed. Hitler called off Operation "Sealion." Churchill spoke for the whole nation when he gave thanks to the fighter pilots: "Never in the field of human conflict was so much owed by so many to so few (144)."

The invasion scare was over. Britain could only be attacked by a war of attrition. London was bombed every night until 2nd November, and then a little less intensely as some bombers were diverted to the Provinces. There were daylight raids too. One diarist wrote: "We are getting quite accustomed to seeing aerial dog fights take place over the capital in broad daylight (145)." The whine of the air-raid warning became part of everyday life. It was reported by an American journalist that, "The siren is not one siren, but many. The sirens are all over the city. They do not stop and start all at once. One starts and just as it gets under way another picks up the note. And then another and another until the whole city is echoing." He described, too, the searchlights which every night "shot straight up. Hard fountains of light that seemed to dissolve into infinity . . . They kept feeling around the sky (146)."

A Member of Parliament wrote in his diary: "Night after night, night after night, the bombardment of London continues . . . Every morning one is pleased to see one's friends again (147)." And every morning London had changed. Graham Greene described "the untidy gaps between the Bloomsbury houses—a flat fireplace half-way up a wall, like the painted fireplace in a cheap doll's house, and lots of mirrors and green wall-papers (148)." Similar sights inspired the poet T. S. Eliot (149):

> Ash on an old man's sleeve
> Is all the ash the burnt roses leave.
> Dust in the air suspended
> Marks the place where a story ended.
> Dust inbreathed was a house—
> The wall, the wainscot and the mouse.
> The death of hope and despair
> This is the death of air.

Kingsley Martin arrived in the West End of London "to find a *Ruined* substantial chunk of Peter Robinson's [store] littering Oxford *buildings* Circus. But Lewis's is the most spectacular. It stands like the ruins of a Greek Temple; a few wide arches and little more (150)." Few public buildings escaped damage. The *Daily Express* printed a picture showing "a gaping hole in the roof of St. Paul's, east of the dome. Nazi raiders have hit the Mother Church of the Empire at last. The bomb smashed down, wrecking the High Altar ninety feet below (151)." Fifteen of Christopher Wren's other churches, the Law Courts and the Houses of Parliament, all suffered direct hits. Harold Nicolson went "to see the ruins of the old Chamber. It is impossible to get through the Members' lobby which is a mass of twisted girders. So I went up to the Ladies Gallery and then suddenly—there was the open air (152)."

The destruction spread beyond the City and West End of London. When one writer moved to a northern suburb later in the war, "only one other house in the road was inhabited. Behind us a long crescent of over a hundred huge empty villas was slowly disintegrating . . . It was an eerie street to go along, with some of its ornate houses lying flat in their own gardens (153)." And in the East End

45

another writer drove to "the other side of Bow Bridge ... the car suddenly reaches a square half-mile of devastation. All life, all semblance of human habitation has disappeared from these crushed and flattened acres (154)." Dylan Thomas commemorated the children killed in these raids (155):

> Secret by the unmourning water
> of the riding Thames
> After the first death, there is no other.

After the salvage operation had dealt as far as possible with the dead, and the damage from the night's inferno, daily life went on surprisingly calmly. "Business as usual," was the rule. Two days after Selfridges department store was bombed, its customers received a letter which stated: "If by any chance you were put to any inconvenience, we feel sure you will appreciate that the circumstances were beyond our control, but we are happy to inform you that every department in the store is now functioning quite normally (156)." A journalist was astonished that "no one in London ever pays any attention to daylight raids, unless he is on the street and hears the plane directly overhead, or sees it diving towards him (157)."

Business as usual

The roof-spotting system helped to localize the warnings and prevent disruption of the whole city at once. A writer described the task of the spotters on the roof of each large factory or office block: "Their job is to stand there and to warn the workers below when danger is close. What is called a 'double red' is then announced, and a bell rung, and the men go to shelter (158)."

Like Selfridges, and the Windmill Theatre—who proudly boasted, after the war, "We Never Closed"—most businesses and factories carried on as usual. In spite of the tension and weariness caused by sleepless nights, one worker wrote: "There was very little absenteeism caused by the raids; in part because we all felt that the raids gave an added importance to our work, but much more because we knew that if we didn't turn up our mates would be worrying. You would see men staggering at their work from lack of sleep (159)." The pertinacity of the women workers impressed J. B. Priestley. He commended "the continued high courage and resolution, not only of the wives and mothers, but also of the crowds of nurses, secretaries, clerks, telephone girls, shop assistants, waitresses who, morning after morning, have turned up for duty as

47

Facing page. Top Firemen fighting fires in Oxford Street, London, after air raids. *Left* These boys lived, but their home was blitzed. *Right* A homeless family stays with friends across the road

neat as ever (160)."

Other women made their contribution through the Women's Voluntary Service, or W.V.S. Stella, Marchioness of Reading, had started the W.V.S. in 1938. Enrolment had increased after Munich to 32,000. Members helped to organize the evacuation of children; they knitted socks for soldiers returning from Dunkirk; they escorted aliens to their internment camps; and, they even made "Molotov cocktails" to throw at the expected German tanks. A journalist unkindly described them "in an unbecoming green uniform . . . loading up a trailer to go to the scene of last night's bombings . . . They reminded me of the housewives of a small village preparing a light refreshment for a charity bazaar (161)." Indeed, many were such country housewives. The same journalist admitted the value of their work in the blitz, when they did everything "from driving ambulances to running canteens, which drive from bombing to bombing bringing warm drinks and food to the A.R.P. workers there (162)."

Public morale Winston Churchill told the nation that Hitler expected to "terrorize and cow the people of this mighty imperial city . . . Little does he know the spirit of the British nation, or the tough fibre of the Londoners (163)." The wartime bravery and humour of Londoners have become mythical. But although they were able to carry on "as usual," they were under enormous strain. Americans were told that, "the individual's reaction to the sound of falling bombs cannot be described. The moan of stark terror and suspense cannot be encompassed by words (164)."

Churchill's broadcasts themselves helped to strengthen morale, as did his visits to blitzed areas. The American Ambassador in London told President Roosevelt: "The Prime Minister's method of conducting a campaign on what one might call a morale front is unique. He arrives at a town unannounced, is taken to the most seriously bombed area, leaves his automobile and starts walking through the streets without guards. The news of his presence spreads rapidly by word of mouth, and before he has gone far, crowds flock about him and people call out to him 'Hello, Winnie,' 'Good old Winnie' (165)."

Provincial blitz Churchill and King George VI travelled out of London to visit the scenes of destruction. At the end of October, 1940, the *Luftwaffe* began to bomb the provinces. The Midlands suffered first. The King went to Coventry and "was horrified at the sight of the centre of

Winston Churchill sees for himself the bomb damage in Liverpool's
Merseyside

the town. The water, electricity and gas services had ceased to
function. I talked to members of the emergency committee who
were quite dazed by what they had been through . . . I walked
among the devastation (166)."

Southampton, Bristol and Birmingham were badly hit. The
Luftwaffe then flew further north. One writer had "seen no ruins
so spectacular as those in Sheffield (167)." During the Liverpool
Merseyside May raids 70,000 people lost their homes. Plymouth
suffered five terrible consecutive nights of raids. A Member of
Parliament wrote in his diary: "The new Home Secretary is worried
about the effect of the provincial raids on morale. He keeps on
underlining the fact that people cannot stand this intensive bombing
indefinitely (168)."

Left A bomb blast has smashed the windows of these London homes, and *Right* plunged a Birmingham shopping district into chaos

The Home Secretary, Herbert Morrison, underestimated the people's capacity. There was panic in Plymouth, but a few months later a journalist reported: "The British at war are very adaptable and already Plymouth has opened new shopping centres (169)." In Sheffield, "when the Blitz was at its height with the houses next door on fire a little Yorkshireman came to the back door. 'Can I borrow your stirrup-pump—they've got a bit of a fire next door.' He might have been borrowing a cupful of milk . . . About 1,080 bombs dropped in that area that night (170)."

Incendiary bombs   Incendiary bombs and fires were the worst hazard. The public were told to "leave a bucket of sand outside your front door, give a key to your warden, [and] leave him a plan showing him where in the house you and your family sleep. Thousands can be rescued from bomb and fire that way (171)." Anna Freud showed her visitor the typical precautions at her home: "Outside the door you must have noticed the pail of sand and the little galvanized-iron scoop . . . The sand is to put out incendiary bombs. The scoop to put on the sand or pick up the bomb before it gets hot (172)."

The firemen became the heroes of the day. But the service was

50

badly strained. Eight hundred people lost their lives and seven thousand were badly injured. They needed help from the public; the government introduced compulsory fire watching. Every man between sixteen and sixty years' old took their turn for forty-eight hours each month. Ernest Bevin announced: "We have adopted the great democratic principle that everybody must become fire watchers, either at their works, their office or on their street (173)." Members of Parliament took their turn at the House of Lords where the Commons were now sitting. When Harold Nicolson dined with an editor of the *New Statesman,* he "went on to sit with him in the N.S. offices as it was his night for fire watching (174)."

Rural safety

Many people packed a few belongings each night and left the towns for the surrounding safe countryside. Thousands "trekked" out of Plymouth during the Spring raids. The countryside was too far away for most Londoners, but during the first days of bombing Epping Forest in Essex became a nightly camping ground. The habit was given up as shelters became more generally used. The government's plans for shelters were not geared to a long onslaught. The trench shelter—the grassy mounds are still visible in the parks— had not been built with night raids in mind. A journalist reported after Munich that "designs for an emergency trench to accommodate six persons, which can rapidly be made in a garden, have been prepared at the Home Office ... The trench should be ten feet long. It should be covered with corrugated iron, or old planks resting on sandbags, or sacks filled with the earth which has been excavated (175)."

But not everybody had gardens; and those who accepted the government's offer of this free Anderson shelter, found it most uncomfortable. Bernard Kops spent a night with his sister "in Stepney Green [London]. We sheltered in her Anderson in the garden. It was terrible in there. I shivered one moment and sweltered the next (176)."

Underground station shelters

The people found their own shelters in the underground stations, not realizing how little protection they would give against a direct hit, or the dangers from flooding. The Kops family, like hundreds of other mothers and children, "in the late afternoon would make for the underground with our bundles of blankets. For every day we had to claim our few feet of concrete. The constant worry was whether we would find a space for that night. We lived

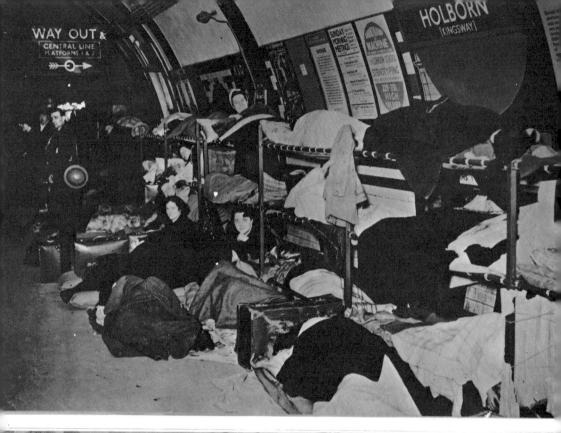

only for four o'clock when they let us down (177)."

As soon as the queue was let into the tube every available space was taken. The night one reporter went into Liverpool Street tube, "you could not have got another human being into it without laying him directly on top of some other human being. This goes for the people lying back against the curving sides of the tube, and for the people flat out along the floor (178)."

A journalist commented: "The government were caught unaware by the rush of people to find room in the tubes. Now, let the people stay. Why not make a good job of it? Bunks, canteens, sanitation first—and after that a system of registering so that numbers can be controlled (179)." The *Daily Express* shelter campaign brought pressure on the government. In October, 1940, Herbert Morrison became Home Secretary, with Ellen Wilkinson as his junior Minister. The domestic shelter which took Morrison's name—a wire and steel contraption under a steel table top—was an improvement on the Anderson shelter. The press reported: "Ellen Wilkinson has begun her job . . . Last night she went round the East End, talking to people, getting out their problems (180)."

Morrison shelters

By the Spring the tube shelters had been improved. Another journalist wrote: "One does not pretend that conditions are entirely satisfactory, but those of us who were familiar—physically sickened —with the cesspool conditions of September can testify to the immense advances which have been made (181)." They became an accepted part of life. Graham Greene's hero "woke, and the sirens were sounding the All Clear. One or two people in the shelter sat up for a moment to listen, and then lay down again. Nobody moved to go home: this was their home now. They were quite accustomed to sleeping underground; it had become as much part of life as the Saturday night film, or the Sunday service, had ever been (182)."

In the mornings, however, after emerging from the shelters, many people found they had no homes to go to. A Ministry of Information advertisement appeared in the press: "What do I do if my home is made uninhabitable by a bomb? I ask a warden or a policeman to direct me to the allotted rest centre (183)." The rest centres were uncomfortable, partly by design to discourage long stays. The Minister of Health told Members of Parliament: "It is an important part of the whole policy that these centres should be kept as clear as possible, that people should stay for as short a period as possible

Rest centres

53

(184)." The government refused the authorities enough money for blankets and food. A report described the "dim figures in dejected heaps on unwashed floors in total darkness: harassed, bustling, but determinedly cheerful helpers distributing eternal corned beef sandwiches and tea—the London County Council's panacea for hunger, shock, loss, misery and illness (185)."

Two hundred thousand people used the rest centres, in spite of the taint they carried of poor law charity. This feeling disappeared in the Autumn when the government itself took over the financing of the centres from the local authorities. A special commission was set up to deal with salvage and rehousing. The press reported that "Mr. Henry Willink, appointed with dictator powers to look after the people of London who lose their homes in air raids, proposed to set up many more rest centres and to improve those already established (186)."

Welfare meals   So the government took responsibility for the welfare of the blitzed. The Ministry of Food set up emergency services in 148 towns to supply hot meals. Rich and poor alike needed sanctuary and food. Calling for an extension of the school meals service, three Ministers told the War Cabinet: "There is no question of capacity to pay: we may find the children of well-to-do parents, and the children of the poor, suffering alike from an inability to get the food they need (187)." The new welfare services were free from social discrimination. The bombs had no respect for class, and broke down many social inhibitions and barriers. Neighbours took each other into their homes. The W.V.S. ladies in the rest centres, and the debutantes nursing in the hospitals, saw real poverty and distress. Humphrey Jennings, making his documentary films, said, "I'm really beginning to understand people and make friends with them."

Class bitterness   But this was only half the story. In some ways the blitz, like evacuation, did more to highlight inequalities than to break down class barriers. George Orwell was bitter: "The bombed-out populations of the East End go hungry and homeless while wealthier victims simply step into their cars and flee to comfortable country houses (188)." When the bombing began there was anxiety lest the suffering, the inadequate shelters and rest centres, and the resentment against the wealthy, would cause revolt against the government. Harold Nicolson noted in his diary that, "Everybody is worried about the feeling in the East End where there is so much bitterness. It is said that even the King and Queen were booed the other day when they visited the destroyed areas. Clem [Davies] says that if only the Germans had had the sense not to bomb west of London Bridge, there might have been a revolution (189)."

As Orwell wrote, "What amounted to a revolutionary situation existed in England, though there was no-one to take advantage of it (190)." Kingsley Martin described "the early days of the shelter committees when the Communists tried to 'nobble' them (191)." But the Nazi-Soviet pact had lost the Communist Party many members. While the Communists denounced the war as imperialist, they could scarcely deny that Nazi Germany was just as wicked, just as capitalist. They were forced into a neutral position. Arthur Horner, the Communist President of the South Wales Miners' Federation, told a journalist: "I am against capitalism, wherever it is. If Hitler is overthrown, it will have to be from inside Germany (192)." *Communist party*

Support for the government and the war was too strong for the Communists to make much headway. The People's Convention was organized by the Party in January, 1941, ostensibly to demand better shelters; but its real purpose was to denounce the war. It attracted over two thousand people. But Claud Cockburn, a Party member, thought it "almost totally futile (193)." The largest Communist demonstration—the occupation of the Savoy restaurant in London, used as a shelter—was a fiasco. There was no popular outcry when the *Daily Worker* was banned for undermining confidence by its dramatic reports of air raids in the provinces.

Hitler's attack on Russia in June, 1941, ended the Communists' opposition to the war. It also ended the British people's fear of the Party. This fear was typified by J. B. Priestley's fictitious works manager, who said that one of his men had "always been on our dangerous list—he's a Communist (194)." Orwell commented that, "By June, 1941, Stalin had come to appear as a very small bogey compared with Hitler (195)."

The British were desperate for an ally. In February, Rommel had gone to the support of the Italians in North Africa, and won back all the gains made by General Wavell the previous December. In the Spring British forces had been forced to withdraw, after a disastrous campaign, from Greece and Crete. The Russian entry into the war was greeted with jubilation. Lord Beaverbrook announced *Russian alliance*

55

An English soldier and his girl friend see an official poster about the Russian alliance: "The Red Army's Fight is *Your* Fight!"

a "Tanks for Russia" week: "Come then, in the foundries and forges of Britain, in the engine works and the assembly lines, to the task and duty of helping Russia to repel the savage invaders who bring torment and torture to mankind (196)." Under the pictures of "Uncle Jo" (Stalin) which took their places beside those of Churchill in the factories, tanks were produced at record speed. One of Evelyn Waugh's characters asked 'Heard the results of Tanks for Russia Week?' 'Well, it's worked' said Box Bender. 'Production was up twenty per cent—and they were supposed to be working all out before.' (197)."

The Russian ambassador's wife named the first tank *Stalin*. Rubber, boots, wool and tin were also sent to Britain's new ally. The economic burden was high but the relief enormous: German planes were needed for Russia; the pressure on London was relaxed and the blitz was over. Intensive bombing gave way to sporadic "tip-and-run" raids until the provincial *Baedeker* raids of 1942. Two and a half million had lost their homes; 43,000 had been killed; 17,000 more were to die during the next four years. But the worst of the civilian suffering was over.

5 Austerity

THE WAR of attrition was fought at sea as well as in the air. In *War of attrition* December, 1940, a journalist reported: "In his last frank and fearless review of the course of the war, the Prime Minister referred to the 'disquieting level' of the sinkings of merchant shipping . . . the average for the whole war has risen to sixty-three thousand tons a week (198)." Ships on the Australian and Asian routes were forced round the Cape because the Mediterranean was closed to them. German U-boats and bombers operated from the French Atlantic coast. Convoys were slow; the Air Ministry was loath to spare precious bombers for their protection. Between March and May, 1941, U-boats sunk 142 merchant ships, and German bombers accounted for 179 more.

In 1940 the British population had not been severely deprived of *Food cuts* food and necessities. An observer in the north commented: "There's no shortage of food evident on Tyneside . . . In Newcastle it's said you can have all the food you want (199)." But the Battle of the Atlantic brought a drastic reduction of five million tons of imports. Lord Woolton, the Minister of Food, "on the subject of eggs . . . said that on one night we lost fifty-five per cent of our supplies for the rest of the war (200)." The meat allocation was reduced from 2s 2d to 1s 2d a week, or just over half a pound. Rationing which had begun so slowly was gradually extended. The rest of the week's allowance was 1 oz. of cheese, 2 oz. of tea, 4 oz. of bacon or ham, 8 oz. of sugar and 8 oz. of fats. Shell eggs were controlled, and one packet of dried eggs allowed each month. Jam and some tinned foods were rationed on a points system.

Despite Churchill's opposition, a similar system was adopted for *Clothing coupons* clothes. Each item cost so many of the sixty-six coupons allotted to everyone each month. One journalist described his ration book: "It was about four inches by six inches, printed on cheap paper, and contained a dozen or more leaves. After a page or two of instructions, it consisted of solid pages of small coupons, the coupons on each page successively labelled sugar, butter, cooking fats, bacon, meat. The instructions told me to pick out the tradesmen with whom I wanted to do business and to register with them, and to inscribe their names in blank places. Then each day in my shopping, these tradesmen were to tear out the coupons necessary to cover my purchases (201)."

J. M. Keynes

The extension of rationing was one aspect of the government's new economic measures. The great fear was inflation. Soon after war broke out the *Times* published two articles by the economist J. M. Keynes. Keynes pointed out that, "More men will be employed, and sometimes at a higher grade of work than that to which they are accustomed . . . It follows that the purchasing power of the working class will command in the aggregate substantially more goods than before (202)." Too much money would be chasing too few goods, the classic condition for inflation.

Rationing alone would not cut down total purchasing power: "It merely serves to divert demand from the rationed to the unrationed article (203)." Other measures would be needed. The war of attrition made it clear that the struggle would not only be a long one, but would involve the daily life of the whole nation. Total war must be fought on a total economic front, with the government having total control of the economy.

Austerity budget

Keynes was a Treasury adviser. His influence on Kingsley Wood's budget of April, 1941, was obvious. His remedies for depriving the people of their extra consumption power, and so avoiding inflation, were first to allow prices to rise a little. The Chancellor announced his intention to stabilize the cost of living index at twenty-five per cent above pre-war level. Government food subsidies, brought in at the start of the war as a temporary measure, would be continued to stabilize this level. Keynes said that more money should be taken away in taxation: "Taxation . . . must involve taxation of the working classes. Three fifths of the expenditure on consumption is by those whose incomes are less than £250 a year, and it is this class whose incomes are likely to rise (204)." The budget created four million new tax payers by lowering the exemption rate to £110 per year. The standard rate of

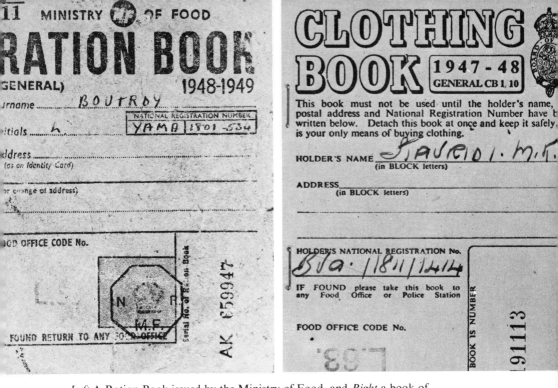

Left A Ration Book issued by the Ministry of Food, and Right a book of coupons needed to buy clothes

income tax went up to ten shillings in the pound.

Part of the money collected in taxes would be repaid after the war in "post-war credits." Keynes had wanted to distinguish between "two kinds of money rewards for the present effort— money which can be used to provide immediate consumption, and money the use of which must be deferred until the emergency is over, and we again enjoy a surplus of production resources . . . It makes all the difference in the world, to each individual personally, whether the excess of his income over his consumption is taken from him by tax or by loan (205)." *Postwar credits*

Side by side with his compulsory saving, voluntary schemes helped to reduce spending. An observer wrote: "The increase in the number of families saving either through savings groups, savings certificates or banks, has been remarkable . . . The savings groups are organized in factories and other places of employment, as well as in schools and in streets. A vast amount of work largely voluntary, has gone into the National Savings campaign (206)." In London, National Savings posters were plastered over the concrete pyramid protecting the statue of Eros in Piccadilly Circus, *Savings* over the plinth of Nelson's column, and over many other public buildings and hoardings. In 1943 they were joined by large pictures of the "squanderbug," a hideous creature wearing swastikas and captioned, "Wanted—for Sabotage." By 1944, £1,075 millions had been saved from personal income.

Queueing   The public responded well to the voluntary savings schemes. They accepted enforced saving and higher taxation. Money and tax problems took second place when each night brought the physical fear of bombs, and each day the struggle of food shortages. Long queues for unrationed goods became a regular part of everyday life. One woman told "how she joins all the queues she sees, not knowing half the time what she is queueing up for. She stands there and after a while whispers to her neighbour: 'What are we queueing for?' (207)." According to a journalist's one day investigation: "Most of the queues took about forty-five minutes to pass through. One queue contained 120 women lined up to get one pound of new potatoes each. In another, a woman stood for nearly three hours and came away with half a pound of tomatoes, the potatoes having gone before her turn came (208)."

American Lend-Lease   Food shipments from America eventually reduced the shortages. In February, 1941, the Prime Minister told President Roosevelt in a radio broadcast, "Give us the tools and we will finish the job." The President's Lend-Lease Act of the next month allowed the United States "to sell, transfer title to, exchange, lease, lend or otherwise dispose of (209)" any article to any government whose defence was considered vital to the safety of America. Britain could buy American goods without having to pay cash. In May, the first shipments of dried eggs, evaporated milk, bacon, cheese and tinned meat arrived.

A Member of Parliament wrote in his diary, "A Minister says that the Lease and Lend Bill is probably the decisive fact of the war, and he is sure that America will be in the war before long (210)." Others feared it would be a substitute for intervention. Americans were told that, "There was no dancing in the streets when the Lend-Lease Act was passed . . . You must understand that the idea of America being of more help as a non-belligerent than as a fight-

Atlantic Charter   ing ally has been discarded (211)."

Throughout 1941 resentment against America's failure to enter the war increased. The Russians were not expected to hold out long

against the German armies. Their defeat would mean an enormous increase in Hitler's economic power, and a desperate need for a new ally. In August, Churchill met President Roosevelt at Placentia Bay. He received a declaration of international principles in the form of the Atlantic Charter, but no promise of intervention. *Pearl Harbour*

The Japanese attack on Pearl Harbour in December, 1941, at last brought America into the war. Germany and Italy declared war on the United States, Britain on Japan. The struggle had become world wide. Britain had the great economic and military force of America behind her, but the immediate effect of Pearl Harbour was to add to her difficulties. German U-boats could now use American waters and do even more damage to British shipping. In 1942 Britain received only twenty-five million tons of imports as opposed to thirty millions in 1941. In Malaya the British retreated; in Hong Kong on 8th December they surrendered. Two days later the Japanese bombed two British battleships, the *Prince of Wales* and the *Repulse*. The loss of great ships always had an appalling effect on morale at home. A Member of Parliament wrote in his diary: "The House is depressed . . . I have a feeling that our nerves are not as good as they were and that we are tired and depressed . . . The loss of the *Prince of Wales* has numbed our nerves (212)." *"I make no promises"*

Winston Churchill returned from his visit to President Roosevelt —who had allayed his fears that America would only fight in the Far East and not in Europe—to face a censure motion in the House. He told Members of Parliament: "I offer no apologies, I offer no excuses; I make no promises . . . (213)." He won his vote of confidence by 464 votes to one. But morale was low throughout the country. J. B. Priestley described the atmosphere "in late January, 1942, with the Japs swarming nearer and nearer Singapore, temporary stalemate in Libya, no bombing of Germany because of the weather and a general feeling of uneasiness and disillusion . . . Queues here and there outside the shops with the black-out waiting just round the corner (214)." The disasters continued. On 12th February two German battleships, the *Scharnhorst* and the *Gneisenau*, sailed calmly and unassailed through the English Channel. The humiliation was keenly felt. Three days later, 15th February, 1942, Singapore fell to the Japanese. George VI wrote to his mother Queen Mary: "I am very depressed over the loss of Singapore and the fact that we were not able to prevent the German ships from getting through the Channel (215)." *German naval power*

Housewives spent long hours queueing for a little food

The King's depression was shared by his people. So many reverses brought not only humiliation but much personal suffering. One writer's experience was typical of many. She described "the sinking of H.M.S. *Prince of Wales* and H.M.S. *Repulse*. Two of our greatest friends were in those ships. Dick survived and wrote me a letter describing his thoughts as he waited in the water to be rescued. Then he was lost in the fall of Singapore. His young widow who had only known a few weeks of marriage, pined and died. Meanwhile we waited months for our other great friend to turn up; but he never did (216)."

Churchill tried to lift everyone's spirits. He spoke over the radio after the fall of Singapore: "Here is another occasion to show ... that we can meet reverses with dignity and with renewed accession of strength. We must remember that we are no longer alone ... Let us move forward steadfastly together into the storm and through the storm (217)." But Churchill was under pressure and forced to reconstitute his war cabinet. Clement Attlee became Deputy Prime Minister, and Sir Stafford Cripps came in as Lord

Privy Seal and Leader of the House.

Sir Stafford Cripps was just the man to introduce the necessary austerity measures as he was devoutly religious with a stern sense of duty. He was also a vegetarian and a teetotaller. He told the House: "Personal extravagance must be eliminated, together with every other form of wastage, small or large, and all unnecessary expenditure (218)." Churchill was somewhat horrified. He told Frederick Lindemann, the scientist and head of his personal statistical staff, "I deprecate the policy of 'misery first' (219)." *Stafford Cripps*

But Cripps put his beliefs into practice. A whole new range of foods including rice, breakfast cereals and biscuits were put on points. The war in the Far East cut off supplies of tea, rice and raw materials, such as rubber and tin. Diets were meagre. At J. L. Hodson's fictional A.R.P. post, the wardens "discussed many subjects but rations were unfailing. Harry Makepeace thought they were a poor 'do.' 'A man can't work the same if he hasn't got meat in his stomach.' 'Some chaps were working at the coal face wi' nobbot bread and marge in their bait cans' (220)."

The shortage of flour brought the end of the white loaf. The pre-war extraction rate of the wheat berry had been seventy per cent. Thirty per cent had been discarded. The Ministry of Food in March introduced an eighty-five per cent minimum, which meant a dark wholemeal loaf. Like the cutting down of sugar consumption, this in fact meant a healthier diet for many people. George Orwell thought that "on average people are better nourished than they used to be . . . I can't help feeling that people in London have better complexions than they used, and that one sees less grossly fat people . . . With an adult milk ration of three pints a week, milk consumption has actually increased since the war (221)." *Food policies*

The Ministry of Food led a campaign against food wastage. The press was full of reports such as that of the woman who was fined ten pounds "for permitting bread to be wasted . . . she was twice seen throwing bread to birds in the garden, and she admitted that bread was put out every day (222)." One of Graham Greene's characters "sprinkled some crumbs over his old brown hat and a flock of sparrows landed there. 'Strictly illegal,' he said, 'I dare say. If Lord Woolton knew' (223)." The Minister's flair for publicity meant that everyone ate "Woolton Pie"—a pie made of vegetables and potatoes. Official recipes for lentil roast, carrot tart and corned beef rissoles which were made with National wheatmeal bread- *Woolton Pie*

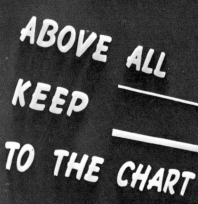

crumbs and "reconstituted eggs," appeared in the press. A. P. Herbert described his delight on a train journey when he was actually offered a real egg (224):

> *Expecting little, demanding naught*
> *Ready to suffer as a good citizen ought;*
> *Ready to hear with a quiet brow*
> *"We did have kippers but we have none now;*
> *A bomb fell on the porridge and the peas;*
> *You should have come last week when there was cheese."*
> *Instead he said "bacon and eggs"*
> *Casual cool, as though it were the rule.*

A diarist wrote: "The weather is now wintry. In spite of this Lord Woolton had decided to reduce our meagre rations of cooking fats ... This will make it all the more necessary for us to dine out. Frying anything is out of the question. Even grilling is difficult (225)." And dining out was limited by Woolton's imposition of a five shillings maximum price for a restaurant meal. Restaurants with high overheads could put in a claim to charge more. Many evaded the order by charging higher prices for wine.

An American journalist remarked: "Every time I have a meal with Ministers and Under-Secretaries, we have fared extremely well. My house has had no sugar for three days. Last evening my meal was onions and potatoes. Nor need I fare so meagrely myself if I care to slip into London and spend money. I lunched with Lady Rhondda at a Soho restaurant on Tuesday. We had a capital lunch with a little red wine, but the cost was twenty-eight shillings. This is all right for me, but not much use to a poor housewife in the suburbs or to the driver of a bus (226)."

But the five shillings limit was generally enforced. Cheaper and nutritious meals were provided by British Restaurants, a service *British restaurants* which was dreamed up by Churchill after the blitz and run by Local Authorities. Over two thousand such restaurants were open by the Autumn of 1943. They were housed in any available building, including a Turkish bath, a millionaire's Park Lane Flat, and the Fishmongers' Hall. They introduced the self-service system in order to save labour. The same journalist who had complained of Woolton's cuts met a friend "who now does voluntary work at the communal restaurant in Chiltern Street. She says you get mulligatawny soup, a plate of roast beef worthy of Simpsons, sprouts and

Facing page "Let your shopping help our shipping!" Government campaigns urged housewives not to waste the food so perilously imported across the sea

potatoes, treacle pudding, cheese, butter and bread, not to mention coffee, all for eleven pence (227)." Bevin's factory canteens also helped to ensure that everyone was well fed in spite of the food shortages.

Domestic articles   Sir Stafford Cripps brought in soap rationing in February, 1942. The production of all household articles was severely restricted. "For a long time razor blades were unobtainable, now it is boot polish (228)," wrote George Orwell. One of J. L. Hodson's characters asked another if he had managed to get a pram for his new baby: "Nay, the firm as were makin' prams 'as turned on to battleships or summat. Might as well try for a Rolls Royce (229)." Production of crockery was limited to a specified plain white range including cups without handles. George Orwell complained of the "hideous white 'utility' hardware, the sort of thing you would expect to see in prison (230)."

Utility articles   The standardization in fact brought in some good plain designs. Furniture design, too, improved after August, 1942, when experts were asked to produce basic "utility" articles. Manufacturers were restricted to these specified standards of design and timber content. Old furniture was impossible to replace except by paying high prices in the second hand shops, or by such methods as one writer described during the blitz: "Into our garden had been blown a broken lawn sprinkler which we converted into a standard lamp . . . From other gardens, sometimes digging a little to unearth them, I collected curtain-rods and rings, and other things needed but impossible to buy (231)."

Clothes   Clothes, too, bore the "utility" label. The Board of Trade told manufacturers exactly what items to produce. Standardized wool and cotton cloths avoided waste and often improved quality. The *Daily Mirror* announced: "From now on we are going to wear utility clothes. Not because we are burning with a desire to show our patriotism, but just because utility clothes are the best value on the market today. The materials are far, far better than those shown in garments at a much higher price (232)." Further restrictions forbade embroidery, trimmings and trouser turn-ups, and limited pleats, seams and buttonholes.

The clothing coupons allocation was cut to forty-eight a year, which was barely enough to buy one decent outfit. A novelist complained in her diary that "The points go far less way than they did . . . Even the tea cloths are costing coupons, and the flour bags which are free don't dry a thing, but some people are making them into curtains. If my dress coupons have to go on towels, soon I shall be nude (233)." "Make-do and mend" was the current slogan, shabbiness the fashion. Jumble sales became popular. At a Home Guard parade in 1943 Ed Murrow noticed that "some of the women wore wooden-soled shoes. They were dressed in the Spring clothes that were new four to five years ago (234)."

The blitz and material shortages brought new fashion styles. One newspaper carried this article: "Fashion problem of the year: what to wear to an air raid shelter at night . . . the answer is obviously 'warblers'. It is cut all in one piece . . . you step into it, zip it up and you're dressed. It has two roomy hip pockets for torch, cards, any of the oddments you want to take with you (235)." Siren suits at night and trousers during the day became the rule of dress for women. An American was surprised that "one out of every ten women I saw wore trousers. They were not self-conscious and they looked better than I expected they would (236)."

Hats were another piece of feminity that disappeared. Scarves were more suitable for air raids and more economical. The President of the Board of Trade enlisted the Archbishop of Canterbury's help in this economy: "Hats are bound to become scarcer, so much so that we do not even put them on the ration but hope that women, and men, too, will largely give up wearing them . . . But convention yields ground slowly and it would help me very much if you felt able to announce that women could, without impropriety come hatless to church (237)." The Archbishop complied—perhaps in return for the Board of Trade's kindness in raising the allowance of material for church hassocks.

Women attending church without hats, and walking the streets in trousers, made prim members of the population fear a new moral laxity. In fact trousers were very modest wear for diving into Morrison shelters in sudden raids. The unladylike habit of hitch-hiking also became popular when Sir Stafford Cripps put an end to private motoring. Official posters asking, "Is your journey really necessary?" discouraged rail travel. The railways were already over burdened with imports which now had to arrive at West coast ports, and by coal which could no longer be safely carried aboard coastal steamers. The best way to get about was to beg lifts from lorry drivers. Girls not only hitch-hiked but plucked up courage to go into pubs. *The Randolph* at Oxford displayed a

New ways of living

notice saying, "No unaccompanied ladies will be served with drinks." In less pretentious bars the watering of the beer kept neither sex away. A social survey made in 1943 showed that "among women aged under thirty, nine said they were going into pubs more often than before the war for every one who said she was going less (238)."

Morality   Did the war really increase immorality at home? The rising figures for illegitimate births, divorces and venereal disease worried many people. Unmarried women gave birth to 25,500 babies in 1939 and 63,420 in 1945. Most of the women were over thirty years' old and seemed to be having a last fling before settling down to a hum-drum spinsterhood. The rise in the divorce rate at the end of the war was hardly surprising when husbands had been away so long. Many marriages had been made hurriedly at the outbreak of war, and had no chance to become stable. One journalist visited a war factory where, "of forty women working there, thirty-eight have made war marriages. Most of them had a married life that lasted a week. When they see their husbands again they will be almost strangers to each other (239)."

The rise in the number of reported venereal disease cases owed as much to the Ministry of Health's publicity campaign, as to any real increase. Much of the stigma was removed and many came forward for treatment. Foreign soldiers stationed in Britain were unfairly accused of spreading the disease. Forces from the dominions arrived early in the war, as did contingents of Poles.

American   Soon after the Japanese attack on Pearl Harbour, American
G.I.'s   servicemen began to arrive for training, swelling the numbers to one and a half million by 1944. Known as G.I.'s from the words "government issue" on their equipment, they became a dominant feature of wartime Britain. George Orwell found that "even if you steer clear of Piccadilly, it is difficult to go anywhere in London without having the feeling that Britain is now occupied territory (240)." The G.I.'s had plenty of razor blades, cheap cigarettes, the new nylon stockings and chewing gum. "Got any gum, chum?" was the usual plea of children following any American soldier. Women and children appreciated their gifts. But, as Orwell pointed out, there was widespread "grievance in the matter of the soldiers' pay and food . . . the Americans are given imported luxuries which obviously waste shipping space . . . People point out with some bitterness that sailors have to be drowned in bringing this stuff

across (241)."

It was not only the G.I.'s who had more than their fair shares. Many shopkeepers kept goods "under the counter" for their best customers. Others ignored the price controls risking a £100 fine or a three months prison sentence. Racketeers who managed to secure rationed or unrationed food which was in short supply, resold it on the black market for exorbitant sums. A story of the Mayfair businessman who "offered for sale 46,800 tins of canned fruit above the fixed maximum price (242)," was typical of many featured each day in the press. Oranges were sold at the then enormous sum of sixpence each; anyone who had enough money and a small conscience could find where to buy petrol or clothing coupons. *Black market*

In March, 1942, the press announced the government's "uncompromising slash at the black market rats . . . Black market racketeers are to be liable to penal servitude up to fourteen years and stripped of all their loot (243)." Strangers were now suspected not of being spies, but black marketeers. When J. B. Priestley's hero met a suspicious looking character on a train he presumed that "his handsome luggage was crammed with forged clothing coupons and orders for a few hundred eggs (244)."

The nation's resentment against the austerity measures and inequalities was building up by the spring of 1942. At the end of March the *News Chronicle* Gallup Poll found that fifty per cent of the people were dissatisfied with the conduct of the war. The editor commented that the Poll's result showed "a widespread sense of frustration . . . The call everywhere is for action (245)." The call took the form of a demand for a second front in Europe, a landing in France. Lord Beaverbrook's *Daily Express* led the press campaign, and was followed by the *Daily Mirror*: "The best method of defence is to hit the other fellow first . . . We want to shorten the war. If we dawdle and wait to spring, in 1943 there may be no spot free from entrenched Germans upon which we *can* spring (246)." The words: "Second Front Now" were scrawled over many walls. *Public opinion*

Churchill resisted the demand for a second front. But in face of the pressure for action he agreed to launch a new bomber offensive against Germany. Sir Arthur "Bomber" Harris, Chief of Bomber Command since February, and Professor Lindemann, were the leading advocates of this policy (see Chapter 7). The British attack on Lübeck on 28th March, 1942, destroyed half the town. The Germans responded with the so-called *Baedeker* raids on cities of *Raids and reprisals* historic interest. King George VI wrote in his diary: "It is outrageous that the Germans should come and bomb our Cathedral cities and towns like Bath which they know are undefended and contain no war industries, as 'reprisal' raids for what we are doing to their war industries (247)." Other towns, such as Exeter, York, Norwich and Canterbury suffered in the same way during May and June. Civilians lived under blitz conditions, "trekking" and sheltering as other provincials and Londoners had done the previous year.

The hardship and suffering under the new German onslaught added to the growing discontent of the British people. In the *Churchill's* Autumn, 1942, the *Times* had considered that, "So far as any man *position* in the world can be regarded as indispensable, Mr Churchill has earned that much abused title (248)." By May, George Orwell thought, "Churchill's position is very shaky. Up to the fall of Singapore it would have been true to say that the mass of people liked Churchill, but in recent months his popularity has slumped heavily (249)." In June a further disaster for Britain came in North Africa with the fall of Tobruk. Harold Nicolson commented: "If there were any alternative to Winston, he might be severely shaken by this event (250)."

But there was no alternative. The censure motion brought against Churchill was lost by 472 votes to 25. Sir Stafford Cripps resigned from the War Cabinet when his demand for a war planning directorate was vetoed. General Auchinleck's withdrawal to a strong defensive position at El Alamein, and the appointment of his successor, General Montgomery, to the command of the Eighth Army foreshadowed victory in North Africa in November. During the same month the Russians defeated the Germans at Stalingrad. The months of despair were over, the advocate of austerity dismissed. Winston Churchill was invulnerable for the rest of the war.

6 Bureaucracy

THE WAR GAVE the British government more power than it had ever wielded before. Only a month after the outbreak in September, 1939, a press leader warned the people: "The posters on a myriad of hoardings assure us in the largest letters that we are fighting this war for freedom. But Mr. Attlee hit an even larger nail on the head when he said last night: 'In fighting for liberty, let us all be sure that we keep our liberty at home.' We have invested our government ungrudgingly with every power over our lives. We did it to enable them to end the war, and we promptly find ourselves hemmed in by the barbed wire of bureaucracy and surrounded by all the tin Hitlers of Bumbledon. They turned out all our lights. They blackened the trains and delayed them. They shut down Billingsgate and sent fish wandering odorously all over the country. They marched into hotels and ejected the residents to make way for more and more officials. They demanded that business men should read and learn an ever-flowing stream of Statutory Rules and orders (251)."

J. M. Keynes, the advocate of total economic warfare, also realized that, "There is a fatal resemblance between bureaucracies in Moscow, Berlin and Whitehall; and we must be careful (252)." But he strongly denied the charges levelled against him and the government that they were "attempting to apply totalitarian methods to a free community (253)." Intervention in every aspect of life was needed if the war was to be won. The government accepted this responsibility in introducing austerity measures. It was also bound to deal with industry.

An increase in industrial production was vital after the fall of France in 1940. Much valuable equipment had been left behind on the beaches of Dunkirk; and manufacturing processes were often out-of-date. Ernest Bevin told the Commons: "We are paying the price for the last twenty years in allowing our industrial output to rust and rot (254)." Britain stood alone. Hitler's attack on Russia had not yet relieved her from the pressure of the blitz. Neither did the Lend-Lease agreement, made in March, 1941, bring immediate arms from America.

More stringent control was needed of the munitions and related industries: the President of the Board of Trade brought in the Concentration of Industry Order. Thomas Balogh, better known for his advocacy of economic planning in the 1964 Labour government, wrote to the press: "The measures . . . calculated to close down factories which have become redundant, as a consequence of the cut in home consumption of inessential goods, are highly welcome. They will permit the maximum liberation of men and machinery for those industries to be incorporated in the war sector, whose expansion is a vital need (255)."

The out of work The shortage of labour became an even more serious problem than that of obtaining raw materials or factory capacity. In 1939, 1,250,000 people were out of work. Unemployment in Britain had become an accepted fact during the depression of the 1930s, and nobody ever imagined there could be a shortage of manpower. The increase in war production was a boon for the depressed areas. One traveller wrote: "You cannot come to Tyneside after seven months of war without feeling the inspiriting effect . . . this neighbourhood is experiencing something like a minor boom in ships and armaments. At Jarrow you can see men of sixty going off to work again . . . war has given them a fresh lease of work (256)." And soon after the slack of unemployment was taken up, King George VI wrote in his diary: "The question of supply of labour and raw materials is being carefully gone into . . . But it is by no means an easy task with the Military Service Act affecting every man of the age of twenty unless they are in a 'reserved occupation.' Skilled labour is at a premium (257)."

War-workers The first real estimate of need was drawn up by the Manpower Requirements Committee in the Autumn of 1940. A weekly journal commented: "If the government's programme is to be carried out, then at least two million persons must be found for the armed forces and the munition industries in twelve months or less . . . Mr. Bevin is a dictator as Minister of National Service, though he offers only 'leadership' for the industrial millions (258)."

Thus Bevin was criticized for not fully using his rights under the Emergency Powers Defence Bill, which had been extended at the height of the invasion scare. The Bill "vested in the Minister of Labour and National Service, the control and use of all labour by empowering him to direct any person in the United Kingdom to perform any such services as he might specify (259)."

Bevin was loath to use such sweeping bureaucratic powers: "The people in this country do not need to be conscripted in the narrow limited sense, and put under a kind of military control to make them do their duty (260)." With Hitler relentlessly pursuing the war of attrition in the air and at sea, and having the Manpower Committee estimates before him, Bevin had to sacrifice his voluntary principle. Men could not be relied upon to find their way into the vital industries fast enough. Some direction and compulsion was needed. In March, 1941, Bevin's Registration of Employment Order forced women of twenty and twenty-one years' old (later extended to all between eighteen and fifty years' old) and all men over forty-one, who were therefore ineligible for the forces, to register for essential war work.

The previous year, Bevin had persuaded the trade unions to accept the principle of dilution. In other words, two men would carry on the work of three, with the help of unskilled labour. The press had announced that "Agreement for the employment of women workers has at last been reached between the employers and the Trade Unions (261)." Women were quickly accepted as part of the industrial scene. They did particularly well in the aircraft factories, where all the work was light. A writer who took a job in a munitions factory described the "stir when the foreman brought the first batch of women into the shop . . . Steadily their numbers increased . . . At first they were put to do labouring jobs, sweeping the shop, helping the fitters, and all kinds of easy services to accustom them to their new environment (262)." For some the work was a welcome deliverance from domestic service. For others, the repetitive work in factories, badly ventilated because of black-out precautions, was an added burden to a life of "making-do" and queueing.

Both the Ministry of Information and individual firms ran publicity campaigns to attract women into war work. One cartoon story described the pride of a young man home on leave, when he found his girl friend had a job in munitions. An even less enticing

Trade unions

Women workers

73

advertisement appeared in a women's journal: "Do you fear you wouldn't be strong enough to undertake heavy factory work? Wembley Tyre firm runs P.T. classes in work time to strengthen muscles, make them fit (263)." A popular dance tune appreciated the women's effort (264):

> *She's the girl*
> *That makes the thing*
> *That drills the hole*
> *That holds the spring*
> *That drives the rod*
> *That turns the knob*
> *That works the thingumebob.*
> *It's a ticklish sort of job, making a thingumebob*
> *Especially when you don't know what it's for!*
> *But it's the girl*
> *That makes the thing*
> *That drills the hole*
> *That holds the spring*
> *That works the thingumebob*
> *That makes the engine roar*
> *And it's the girl*
> *That makes the thing*
> *That holds the oil*
> *That oils the ring*
> *That works the thingumebob*
> *That's going to win the war.*

In May, 1942, Ernest Bevin told the American ambassador: "The total number of women in industry and the services at the present moment is 6,311,000 (265)." Registration brought in more than five million more men to essential war work. The new system of "protected establishments" saved them from the call-up. When Bevin announced that two out of three people between the ages of fourteen and sixty-four were in the forces, or fully engaged in industry, one newspaper said that the figures "came as something of a shock to most people. No country in the world has ever mobilized its manpower to this extent (266)."

Essential work orders   Once in the vital industries, workers were kept there by Bevin's Essential Work Orders (E.W.O.'s). He explained to the House of Commons: "As the manpower position became more difficult, I came to the conclusion that one of the best ways to deal with it and

War work for women. *Left* Shaping the nose of a shell and *Right* Girls learning how to install electric wiring in battleships

stop the turnover of labour, was to get the industries sorted out. In view of the urgency of the question I began with shipbuilding. I found out how many men could be employed . . . the bulk of those men have been supplied . . . Then I applied the E.W.O. That holds the man to his job (267)." After shipbuilding, E.W.O.'s were applied to engineering, aircraft work, the railways and the building trade.

Bevin's trade union background was invaluable in persuading the unions to accept the E.W.O.'s. Moreover, the Orders were often made conditional on better negotiated wage rates. The dockers were changed from a casual into a permanent labour force, with a guaranteed minimum wage of £4 2s. 6d. Factory workers were given, as well as higher wages, canteen and welfare officers. Also,

Beaverbrook's high hopes

the hours of work were limited.

Lord Beaverbrook's post-Dunkirk drive had resulted in one week's increased production, and then exhaustion. He still tried to fix targets impossibly high, to stimulate effort in the factories. The head of a northern engineering firm told an observer a typical, if apocryphal, story: "Beaverbrook was inspecting a big aircraft factory when he saw a new type of plane. He asked when the plane would be ready, and was told two months. He said it must be up in the air and bombing Berlin in two days. The whole production schedule was disorganized, the assembly lines stripped, everything concentrated on to the plane. By a stupendous effort the plane was ready within two days, flown to the aerodrome and handed over to the R.A.F. The job Beaverbrook asked for had been done, though the production of the factory would be interfered with for weeks after. That night, within forty-eight hours of Beaverbrook's visit the plane went over to bomb Berlin. When the bomb aimer pulled the stick, out fell two members of the night shift (268)."

Beaverbrook could get things done, but in the long run, he did not add to industrial efficiency. Tanks were produced, although rarely with enough spare parts to keep them in action. Churchill supported Bevin in the move against Beaverbrook to cut exorbitant working hours: "If we are to win the war it will be largely by staying power. For that purpose you must have reasonable minimum holidays for the masses of the workers (269)." Beaverbrook lost that particular battle. His tenure of the Ministry of Production, after Churchill's reconstitution of his war cabinet in early 1942, was short lived.

Workers support Bevin

The workers appreciated Bevin's efforts on behalf of their welfare. They responded to his appeal: "You may get your irritations in the factories, but don't you stop work from now on either in mines, factory, dock or anywhere else for one minute. You don't hurt me, you don't hurt the government, but that one minute may mean the life of one of your sons in the fighting field. It is criminal to stop work at this moment (270)." There were few strikes in the first years of the war. The year 1943, however, brought absolutely full employment and therefore absolute security for the workers.

War weariness

During this time, a certain war weariness also overtook the population. Churchill and Roosevelt now agreed at Casablanca that the main war effort should be directed against the U-boats in the Atlantic. Sicily, where the Mediterranean offensive began with allied landings in July, seemed as remote as the Atlantic or the Far East. There little, in any case, was happening. Tip and run raids continued, bringing their own tragedies. But they were not intensive. In 1943 civilians felt less involved in the war than they had done earlier. No longer was there the fear of invasion, the horrors of the blitz or the excitements of the African campaign. Patriotism no longer kept men at work. In 1943 the provincial bus men, the Liverpool dockers and the engineering workers all went on strike.

The worst strikes were in the coal industry. The situation here *Coal industry* was aggravated when Bevin tried to force all men with mining experience back into the pits. A volunteer miner in Nottingham wrote: "Pit after pit ceased work at the threat made by the government to conscript the sons of miners into the pits. Their aim for years had been to persuade their children not to go down the mines, and now they were told that all these young men were to be forced into the pits (271)." The 1941 E.W.O.'s that applied to the mines had been too late to stop the drift of miners going towards the better paid munition factories. One miner commented: "You have men working in this industry where their daughters are working on the other side of the road, and taking £2 a week more than their fathers home in wages (272)."

The shortage of miners meant a severe shortage of coal for the munitions factories. Hugh Dalton, the President of the Board of Trade since Oliver Lyttleton took Beaverbrook's place at Production, wanted to ration coal: "Unless you have a rationing system people whose houses are damaged by bombs . . . and people who are sick will get no special attention. They will just have to join in the scramble and get what they can (273)." But the Conservatives, under pressure from powerful mine owners, vetoed the Bill. Neither an increased minimum wage rate in June, 1942, nor an offer of the pits to conscripts as an alternative to the forces, attracted new miners.

In December, 1943, Bevin told the House of Commons: "I therefore propose to resort to the most impartial method of all, that of the ballot. A draw will be made from time to time of . . . the numbers from 0 to 9 and those men whose national service registration certificates happen to end with the figure will be transferred to coal mining (274)." The unlucky conscripts forced into the mines were called "Bevin Boys." Most of them worked on haulage and maintenance because they were not tough enough for the coal face. A volunteer in the pits wrote: "The miners regarded them with good natured aloofness . . . It would do the Bevin Boys no harm to see what the pits were like, but as for increasing production—a fat lot of difference they would make. Why, it would be more trouble to teach them than to do the work yourself (275)."

Women's land army

Like the mines, the farms lost men to the forces and factories. Bevin forbade other industries to employ agricultural workers, and in 1941 postponed their conscription. He raised their basic wage from thirty-two shillings to forty-eight shillings. But he was too late to stop the flow of men from the land. The land girls, answering the call for volunteers in 1939, took their place. Early suspicions of their ability soon disappeared. After one year, farmers were crying out for them and a journalist admitted: "No one will deny that the nine thousand members of the Women's Land Army now at work have shown themselves capable of understanding a large variety of jobs on the farm . . . Apart from milking and care of livestock, volunteers are normally employed as tractor drivers, shepherdesses, wagoners and general farm hands. Through the severe weather of last winter they carried on manfully. Though in many cases they had to wade through deep snow to their work, they were up at five in the morning, sliding across the yard to milk the cows long before it was light (276)."

Victoria Sackville West wrote, as well as *The Land*, a patriotic song encouraging girls (277):

> *Back to the Land, with its clay and its sand*
> *Its granite and gravel and grit*
> *You grow barley and wheat*
> *And potatoes to eat*
> *To make sure that the nation keeps fit.*

Dig for victory

Import cuts meant more food must be grown at home. Government posters begged everyone to "dig for victory." The press reported: "Food production corps are to be formed by local authorities to turn flower gardens into vegetable gardens (278)." The response was good. Evelyn Waugh described how "the gardeners all over the country . . . ploughed up their finest turf and transformed herbaceous borders into vegetable plots (279)."

Ploughing was the keyword on the farms. The *Times* explained that, "The sole criterion today is food production from the land . . .

Facing page. Top left Ernest Bevin, Minister of Labour, watches a "Bevin boy" in a munitions factory. Top right Life in the Women's Land Army. Bottom left An evacuee boy helps to grow home produce, as urged by the official poster Bottom Right

DIG FOR VICTORY

The all grass farm carrying a stock of ewes and store cattle may be producing only a fraction of the output which could be obtained from the land (280)." One traveller noticed that "Aberdeenshire's increased area under food since the war is fully sixty thousand acres (281)."

Farming policies The Ministry of Agriculture appointed War Agricultural Committees to survey farms and, if necessary, enforce more efficient agricultural methods. As a journalist commented, "It is only on the basis of accurate information about the farms in each district which are badly farmed that effective action can be taken to intensify production (282)." The author of a Penguin Special book, published in 1942, wrote: "Farmers have been compelled to break up their grass fields and sow them with approved crops, but as these include practically everything known to British husbandry and as a price schedule for the produce has been drawn up sufficiently generous to keep even the inefficient of the farming community in business, the new activities required of them have entailed little interference after the initial stage, and no risks, while leaving large profits to the man who knows his business (283)."

Not all farmers were so sure that government interference was a good thing. Some complained that "the Minister of Agriculture is empowered to dispossess any farmer, there being no legal necessity for his giving any particular length of notice, and no need to provide any alternative accommodation (284)." The powers were occasionally abused. A Worcestershire farmer later described how his farm "was taken over by the Worcestershire W.A.C. in May, 1943. I pleaded to be allowed to keep the house for my wife and family. This was refused . . . The Minister of Agriculture has stated that, before any farmer was turned out he was advised, helped, urged and cajoled. We had none of this. We received notice to quit and were turned out (285)."

All farmers resented the introduction of double Summer time for the sake of industry. It was all very well for the industrialist Lord Nuffield to be convinced that it would "make for quicker and less tiring travel between home and factories, reduce absence due to ill health and generally contribute to the maintenance of a high rate of output (286)." But as Bevin pointed out, "The agricultural worker in the field . . . has to turn out in the early morning darkness, and this is accentuated by the prolongation of Summer time (287)."

Working in the factory or on the land, people's lives were regu-

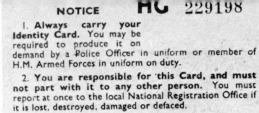

NOTICE

1. **Always carry your Identity Card.** You may be required to produce it on demand by a Police Officer in uniform or member of H.M. Armed Forces in uniform on duty.

2. **You are responsible for this Card, and must not part with it to any other person.** You must report at once to the local National Registration Office if it is lost, destroyed, damaged or defaced.

3. If you find a lost Identity Card or have in your possession a Card not belonging to yourself or anyone in your charge you must hand it in at once at a Police Station or National Registration Office.

4. Any breach of these requirements is an offence punishable by a fine or imprisonment or both.

FOR AUTHORISED ENDORSEMENTS ONLY

51-266

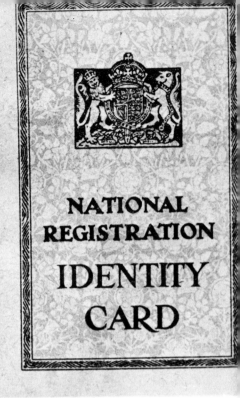

NATIONAL REGISTRATION IDENTITY CARD

Every citizen had to carry an Identity Card like this

lated in every detail. "The man from the Ministry" could knock on any door, ask questions, impose regulations. All ministries grew in size and importance as the war went on. The Ministry of Food operated more than a thousand local offices which issued ration books, identity cards, free orange juice and cod liver oil. It employed 50,000 civil servants. The Ministries were co-ordinated at local level by regional commissioners. The vast bureaucratic system produced grim humour. In Tommy Handley's first radio programme, *Itma (It's That Man Again)* he announced: "They've made me Minister of Aggravation and Mysteries and put me in charge of the Office of Twerps, otherwise known as *Itma*. (Phone rings.) Yes, this is *Itma*. What? You want to take over Peabody Buildings to use as H.Q. for the Ministry of Mothballs? Certainly, take over the whole place immediately. Chuck everybody out (288)." One of Evelyn Waugh's characters, when asked whether some good war songs might not come out of the struggle replied: "I rather doubt it, there's probably a department of martial music at the Ministry of Information (289)."

Rules and regulations

81

Perhaps the famous British sense of humour acted as a safety valve, minimizing resentment against the extended bureaucracy. Many people even welcomed the chance of shelving personal responsibilities. One man was "appalled by the willingness of the evacuees to leave everything to the government (290)." There were many demands for more, rather than less, government intervention. The *Times* received a letter demanding that the government should force people to dig up their gardens (291). Another correspondent wrote during the blitz: "Is it not the plain duty of any occupier of premises to see that his windows are properly protected, or at any rate, treated with a transparent paint which makes them splinter proof? And should not the government make this commonsense treatment compulsory? (292)."

Tolerance of bureaucracy
The ordinary British civilian accepted the bureaucratic system, but he felt divorced from the government which administered it. Churchill might have removed Neville Chamberlain's "old guard" but the gap between the rulers and the ruled remained. One writer was told by a civil servant: "The public are regarded as children from whom knowledge must be kept (293)." The people's chosen representatives had little control over policy or strategy. George Orwell described the House of Commons: "The whole thing now has a mangy, forgotten look . . . the feeling that Parliament has lost its importance is very widespread (294)." Churchill ran the war through his Inner Cabinet; he ran the country through his bureaucratic ministries. But his personal popularity was unaffected by resentments against his bureaucrats. The people bore an unprecedented amount of interference in their private lives with grumbles, but without revolt.

7 Arts and Sciences

Censorship

WHEN THE TIME came to relax with their newspapers or radio, the people of Britain were still not free of bureaucracy. Censorship was imposed by the Ministry of Information. This was partly to prevent useful information, such as the movement of troops, the building of new factories, or even the weather, reaching the enemy. Partly it was to ban any news presentation which might undermine support for the war. J. B. Priestley was taken off the air when his *Postscripts* became too political (see Chapter 3). Michael Redgrave and other entertainers were also warned they would not be allowed to broadcast if they took part in the anti-war People's Convention. When the Emergency Powers Defence Bill had been extended, Ed Murrow told his American listeners: "Any newspaper opposing the prosecution of the war can now be suppressed (295)." The *Daily Worker* was shut down in January, 1941 (see Chapter 4). The *Daily Mirror* was warned that it would suffer the same fate if it continued to attack government, profiteers and luxury restaurants. The Editor wrote: "Several million readers of the *Daily Mirror* will see in our news columns this morning that our newspaper has been threatened with instant suppression. Mr. Herbert Morrison accuses us of a reckless indifference to the national interest (296)."

Paper shortage

However, editors accepted with equanimity the Ministry of Information's defence notices restricting news coverage; few tears were shed when the *Daily Worker* was suspended. For the rest of the war the press suffered less from censorship than from the paper shortage. Imports of timber were falling. Local committees organized salvage drives; the Ministry of Supply called in old books to be pulped. A journalist "on the way down Jermyn

Street ... noticed a stall where old newspapers were being sold at a halfpenny each for wrapping." He added: "Newspapers are now down to 4,000 tons of newsprint a week, from 24,000 tons, and it is not impossible that the newspapers will come down to two pages (297)." Many had boasted of twenty-four pages before the war. The *Daily Express* was made up of twelve pages in 1940 and four in 1941.

Reading boom   Practically everybody had either a relative or friend at sea, or in the forces. The news in the press of a skirmish with U-boats, of an offensive in Africa in 1942, of a landing in the Mediterranean in 1943, was often the first indication of where he might be. More people than ever before read the newspapers. According to the Wartime Social Survey, four out of five men, and two out of three women, bought a newspaper each day. The *Daily Mirror* with its cartoon "Jane," and its columnist, Cassandra, won the circulation battle. But there was little room in the limited number of pages for long general articles. So people turned to books.

Publishers were naturally hit by the paper shortage, too. Harold Nicolson met one: "He talks to me about the difficulty of getting paper for a bestseller he has discovered (298)." But the demand for reading matter was so great that, as Evelyn Waugh wrote: "It was in miniature a golden age for the book trade. Anything sold; the supply of paper alone determined a writer's popularity (299)."

"Anything sold," mainly because there was an element of escapism in the cry for books. Romantic and detective titles were popular. George Orwell complained: "Novels are still being published in great numbers, but they are of a trashiness that passes belief (300)." *No Orchids for Miss Blandish* was a bestseller. The crime writer Agatha Christie was in great demand. Established authors like Graham Greene also flourished. All books, new or secondhand, sold well. A diarist noticed "a bookstall in Oxford Street which offers to buy secondhand books at fifty per cent of the purchase price (301)."

The black-out and the blitz increased the reading habit. "During the dark, interminable evenings, many English families, tired of travelling through the cold blackness to clubs and restaurants, come to know their homes as they have never known them before. Publishers and editors rejoice; these fireside nights will inevitably mean a large increase in reading. The libraries flourish; sixpenny

Penguins with white covers carrying scarlet titles appear in their hundreds on every bookstall, and are eagerly purchased (302)."

Two new monthly magazines, Cyril Connolly's *Horizon* and John Lehmann's *Penguin New Writing* did well. They introduced new writers to the public, including the poet Alun Lewis whose *Raider's Dawn* appeared in 1942:

> *And lovers waking*
> *From the night*
> *Eternity's masters,*
> *Slaves of time—*
> *Recognize only*
> *The drifting white*
> *Fall of small faces*
> *In pits of lime.*
>
> *Blue necklace left*
> *On a charred chair*
> *Tells that Beauty*
> *Was startled there.*

Alun Lewis was a soldier, killed in action in 1944. Yet he preferred to write about air raids than battlefields. Like his fellow soldier poets, Sidney Keyes and Keith Douglas, Lewis accepted war's inevitability: he did not rage against it. For this reason there was a dearth of inspired war poetry to compare with the writings of Wilfred Owen and Robert Graves in the First World War. The best known poets, Edith Sitwell, T. S. Eliot and Dylan Thomas wrote only peripherally about the war. Publishers liked to publish verse, which only used a little precious paper. Poetry reached a growing public. Harold Nicolson went "to the Aeolian Hall for the poetry reading ... I am impressed by Eliot's reading from *The Waste Land* and rather moved by the Poet Laureate [John Masefield] ... Vita recites *The Land* quite perfectly (303)."

A few people went to poetry readings. Many more spent their lunch hours in the early months of the war listening to the pianist Myra Hess. Kingsley Martin announced: "At one o'clock every day except Saturdays and Sundays, and at 4.30 p.m. on Tuesdays and Fridays, there is now music at the National Gallery. Miss Myra Hess, who has organized these concerts, and Sir Kenneth Clark, who has given them a home, deserve our congratulations. Already they must know how grateful we are, for at the first concert there was an audience of a thousand (304)." A social

All British newspapers were censored during the war for security reasons

survey commented that "It was left to the initiative of a single woman to pierce the black-out by producing her own concerts (305)."

C.E.M.A.   At the end of 1940 the government accepted some responsibility for the sad state of the arts after the closing down of concert halls, art galleries and theatres. It supported the Council for the Encouragement of Music and the Arts, which graduated after the war into the Arts Council. With funds from C.E.M.A., orchestras and theatre companies began to play again. The Old Vic theatre, with Sybil Thorndike as its leading lady, travelled to the provinces giving performances of the classics.

E.N.S.A.   Ernest Bevin thought C.E.M.A. "too 'ighbrow." He introduced less intellectual entertainment into the factories. At the outbreak of war the theatrical producer Basil Dean had persuaded the government to support his Entertainments National Service Association for providing shows for the forces. The following Spring the press announced "E.N.S.A.'s intention to inaugurate a series of lunchtime concerts in factories (306)." Few performers had the star qualities of Gracie Fields; E.N.S.A. concerts were often criticized for their low standards.

But J. B. Priestley saw much good in them: "The other day I saw two thousand people push aside what remained of the fried plaice and chips they'd had for lunch, lift their eyes and ears towards an orchestra consisting of four young women in green silk, and then, all two thousand of them, roar out *Oh Johnny, Oh Johnny, How You Can Love*. And having paid this tribute to Johnny and applauded the four young women in green silk, these two thousand people returned—much heartened—to another five or six hours work at their machines. Obviously this genial conspiracy between the Ministry of Labour and E.N.S.A. to provide entertainment during the meal hours for workers in the war factories was a roaring success (307)."

Outside the office and factory, most people found their entertainment in the cinema. A social survey interviewer was told in a munitions factory in 1943: "The pictures is the one event in the week which the factory girls really do look forward to and enjoy (308)." Many of the films they saw were American. Conscription of studio hands and requisitioning of studios cut down home production. The American films like *Song of Bernadette* and *Gone with the Wind*, which played in London's West End for two years, were popular because audiences could escape from their war environment. One diarist went "to see *Moon over Miami* at the Odeon. This is a colour film and is a delightful escape from the war (309)." War films such as *Desert Victory* only became popular after the victories in late 1942.

Cinema

While the numbers of British films were limited, they improved in quality: the industry received an unexpected boost from the government. Its Crown Film Unit, under Humphrey Jennings, was an open exercise in propaganda. But it had a revolutionary effect. Jennings' documentaries introduced a new realism into film making, and foreshadowed such films as *In Which We Serve* and *Brief Encounter*. The American producer, Sam Goldwyn, admitted that "Britain has stopped trying to imitate us. They have begun

Music in wartime. *Left* The pianist Myra Hess plays at one of the London lunchtime concerts which made her famous. *Right* Vera Lynn, the "Forces' Sweetheart."

to use a method of their own, applying a broader viewpoint and getting closer to people (310)." British stars like James Mason, Stewart Granger, Rex Harrison and Margaret Lockwood went to Hollywood later, but they all made their names at home during the war years.

Crooners The other idols in these years before rock and roll and pop singers were the lady crooners. At E.N.S.A. concerts Vera Lynn, the forces' sweetheart, sang:

We'll meet again, don't know where, don't know when,
But I know we'll meet again some sunny day.

Tin Pan Alley, as the music business was known, flourished on the proceeds of this and other songs. They included *Lili Marlene, Shine on Victory Moon* and, most popular of all, *We're gonna hang out the washing on the Siegfried Line.* A song writer admitted: "This is a damn fine war as far as we are concerned (311)." The songs were played over and over again in the dance halls where the *Lambeth Walk* gave way to the *Black-out Stroll* and the *Jitterbug.* When the British Jitterbug Marathon was held in 1940 a journalist commented drily, "Perhaps this noisy exhibition was all in keeping with a mad world in which madmen are conflicting to dominate the continent (312)."

Radio listeners

Vera Lynn could be heard crooning over the wireless at intervals during the day. Before the dance halls and the cinemas reopened after the first months of the war everybody had caught the radio habit. A typical family spent its evening at home listening to a large cumbersome radio set—an odd scene now that the television dominates every living room and a transistor is something to be carried in the pocket. A few people had television sets before the war, but technical development was arrested in 1939. The B.B.C. offered both entertainment and much wanted news. One writer commented at the outbreak of war: "The first thing that happened was the change in the wireless. It gave up being dull . . . bursting into news bulletins every forty-five minutes or so (313)."

As a security measure, news readers were no longer anonymous. Each began, "Here is the news and this is Alvar Liddell" (or Bruce Belfrage, or Stuart Hibberd) "reading it." The familiarity of the names and the unemotional reliable reports did much to keep civilian morale high. One man at least remembered "how, stumbling through the darkness towards one's home, the first real reassurance that the world had not changed its pattern was provided by the quiet, calm, cultivated tones that emerged from the radio receiver (314)."

Fourteen million people listened each week to the Radio Doctor. Dr. Charles Hill (now Lord Hill) advised them in down-to-earth tones how to look after themselves in war time, recommending, "my old friend the dandelion leaf," as a salad. Almost as many heard Tommy Handley's comic programme *It's That Man Again*. *Itma's* catch phrases—"I don't mind if I do," "Can I do you now, sir?" "Don't forget the diver" and T.T.F.N. [ta-ta for now]— became part of the Englishman's vocabulary. They united the nation in a way no government propaganda could do. Colonel Chinstrap and Mrs. Mopp became national characters. The B.B.C., as has been seen, was well aware of its propagandist role and took care not to spread alarm and despondency.

Brains Trust

It also remembered its former puritan Director-General, Lord Reith, and set out to educate as well as entertain. Like the efforts of C.E.M.A., the B.B.C's weekly *Brains Trust* was a genuine and successful attempt to bring both culture and pleasure to the people. Professor Joad, Commander Campbell and Julian Huxley were

89

heard on the programme every week, answering philosophical, scientific or any other questions from the public. "By and large it stood for enlightenment, and that was why millions of listeners welcomed it," wrote George Orwell (315). The *Brains Trust* was so influential that the Archbishop of Canterbury demanded that a Church representative or at least a Christian, should be on the panel. He wrote to the Director-General of the B.B.C.: "Quite a large section regard it as an opportunity for ascertaining the serious views of leading scientists upon questions of the moment, and though the answers are often light heartedly given they are also seriously accepted ... If the Christian, or at least the religious attitude to the universe is not represented, it is by implication denied (316)."

Religion   The Archbishop was worried about the spiritual state of his people. By the beginning of the war Protestantism was already declining. One writer asked: "Has the war resulted in any sort of a religious awakening among civilian people? ... The Bishop of Bradford has seen no signs yet of a religious revival. Religious argument and controversy, yes (317)." Professor Joad described the type of controversy: "In discussions among students there is a widespread tendency to re-open questions to which religion has hitherto provided the answer. Did God will the war? If so how can he be good? Is the war perhaps even a punishment for our sins? (318)." In London society, as well as in the universities, "It is curious what a lively interest most of us have taken in God during these last few weeks. People who hardly knew of his existence before suddenly began to ask each other what God could be thinking about to allow such awful things to happen to the British Empire (319)."

But the questioning did not lead to increased faith, or even increased church attendances. At local level, churches were emptied first by the silencing of their bells, then by bomb damage, and the exodus of old congregations from their homes. Church halls were requisitioned for rest centres and for evacuees' transit homes; many country women who had been the backbone of the village church left for more exciting voluntary work in the W.V.S. Ed Murrow reported: "Organized religion has, on the testimony of some of its own leaders, failed to achieve any substantial advance, and has in some cases lost ground (320)."

90   The church was unsure of its role during the war. Its prelates

argued amongst themselves. William Temple of Canterbury wrote to the Archbishop of York who "often told people not to hesitate to pray for victory." "I am afraid I distress you by the fact that the forms of prayer which I draw up do not contain direct prayers for victory . . . I am of course prepared to say 'Grant us victory if it be Thy will' but I am sure that clause ought to be added (321)."

Many laymen wished the church would keep to its spiritual province. Harold Nicolson wrote in his diary: "B.B.C. Board. We discuss whether the clergy should use the microphone to preach forgiveness to our enemies. I must say I prefer that to the clergy who seek to pretend that the bombing of Cologne was a Christian act. I wish the clergy would keep their mouths shut about the war. It is none of their business (322)." But where morality and politics overlapped, churchmen intervened. While many of them justified Sir Arthur Harris's raids on Lübeck and Rostock in the Spring of 1942, Bishop Bell of Chichester attacked night bombing as "a degradation of the spirit for all who take part in it (323)."

The bombing of Germany was intensified in 1943. In January *Bombing* at Casablanca President Roosevelt and Winston Churchill had agreed that the war should be fought to the bitter end. Their enemies must accept unconditional surrender. The successful Summer campaign in Italy brought Mussolini's surrender. The two premiers also agreed to step up strategic bombing as the best way of forcing Hitler to do the same. The Ruhr suffered in the Spring and Hamburg in the Autumn. The Germans retaliated with the "little blitz" on London and the provinces. A thousand people were killed during seven February raids on London. Berlin suffered even heavier casualties and even worse devastation. One of David Low's cartoons showed a man chivvying his wife who was gazing up at the night sky, bright with searchlights and bombers: "Never mind it not being 'arf what we're giving them—let's git home (324)."

Few British people were particularly vindictive, but six out of ten, according to a Mass Observation survey, gave "unqualified verbal approval" to the bombing of German cities (325). Nearly everyone believed that only military objectives were being attacked. It was left to Bishop Bell to attack the bombing policy even more strongly than before. He spoke in the House of Lords against "the method of area bombing . . . It is no longer definite military and industrial objectives which are the aim of the bombers, but the whole town, area by area, is plotted carefully out. This area is singled out and plastered on one night; that area is singled out and plastered on another night (326)."

Strategic bombing Sir Arthur Harris and the influential Lindemann both sincerely believed that strategic bombing would bring Germany to her knees. Harris wrote: "The main, and almost the only, purpose of bombing was to attack the morale of the industrial workers. This was to be achieved by destroying the whole of the four largest cities of the Ruhr (327)." Lindemann wrote a paper telling Churchill: "There seems little doubt that this would break the spirit of the people (328)." The scientists, Henry Tizard and P.M.S. Blackett, who saw Lindemann's minute to the Prime Minister, doubted its forecast of the effect of area bombardment. Blackett "came independently to the same conclusion as Tizard: I estimated the error as sixfold. The main mistake made in the Cabinet paper was to assume that all bombers which would be delivered from the factories in the next eighteen months would in the same period have dropped all their bombs on Germany (329)."

Bishop Bell pointed out: "It is urged that area bombing will break down morale and the will to fight. It is pure speculation. Up to now the evidence received from neutral countries is to the opposite effect; it is said that the Berliners are taking it well (330)." Contrary to Harris's claim that "We can wreck Berlin end to end . . . It will cost us four hundred to five hundred aircraft. It will cost Germany the war (331)," the bombing neither shattered German morale nor shortened the war by a day.

Lindemann Tizard, Blackett, and Bishop Bell were proved right. Meanwhile, Lindemann's position was impregnable. "Bold men protested to Churchill about Lindemann's influence and were shown out of the room. Before long everyone in official England knew that the friendship was unbreakable and that he had real power (332)." His position, and the importance of his conflict with Tizard in deciding strategy, was symptomatic of the new involvement of scientists in politics and administration. Professor Blackett wrote later that, "During the first years of the Second World War circumstances arose in which it was found that civilian scientists would sometimes play an important role in the study of tactics and strategy (333)."

Radar In one vital area, scientists had already begun to play this role. The Tizard Committee, set up in 1935, sent scientists to the Biggin

Hill fighter station to study methods of air defence. It quickly adopted the ideas of Robert Watson who used Sir Edward Appleton's discovery of radar for detecting and intercepting enemy planes. A chain of radar stations was set up along the south coast. "Cats-Eye" Cunningham, the ace fighter pilot, attributed nearly all his successes to radar (See Chapter 4). The plates of grated raw carrot in the pilots' mess rooms were merely a publicity stunt which was designed to convince potential spies that these successes were due to sharpened eyesight.

Other scientists helped to win the battle at sea. They found the *Mines* answer to the German magnetic mine which was destroying so many British merchant ships during the phoney war: a demagnetizing electric cable was fitted to each ship's hull. Work on the atomic bomb, under the code name Tube Alloys, had to be transferred to America because of labour and material shortages. But without the work done at Birmingham University early in 1940, and its development by the Maud Committee, the bomb could probably not have been produced by 1945.

Despite these successes, a group of scientists complained in a *Wartime* Penguin Special published in the Summer of 1940, of "a lack of *science* effective organization of scientific work . . . A large proportion of the scientific brains in this country are not being used at all and most of those that are being used are not working at anything like their possible efficiency. In dealing with old problems the best use is often not made of existing knowledge. In dealing with new, there is little disposition to initiate and carry out highspeed research (334)."

Pushed by Sir John Anderson who was himself a scientist, Churchill at last recognized the need for scientific research. Blackett described how "In August, 1940, . . . I was invited to become scientific adviser at the headquarters of the anti-aircraft command at Stanmore [Middlesex]. My immediate assignment was to assist service staff to make the best use of the gun-laying radar sets (335)." He was transferred first to Coastal Command and then to the Admiralty. His success in introducing scientific methods, in spite of the early suspicions of the service chiefs, made "operational research" as much an accepted part of the government's war effort as the production of tanks and aircraft.

Research was applied to general strategy and to such vital *Camouflage* details as the camouflage of buildings. Scientists attacked the folly of "the decoration of cooling towers of a large works to represent a grove of tall trees. It should scarcely be necessary to point out that the result of light and shade is such as absolutely to kill this piece of stage scenery from bombing range (336)." In future, scientists—not artists—were made responsible for camouflage. In their laboratories they worked under pressure to discover substitutes for unobtainable raw materials, such as rubber and cotton. They developed plastics and synthetic fibres. Nylon was used in large quantities for parachutes. In the same way, wartime demands of the aircraft industry speeded up the development of the jet engine.

Scientific advisers   In October, 1940, a scientific advisory committee of the Cabinet was set up. Scientists were attached to the various ministries. At the Ministry of Agriculture they introduced new fertilizers to increase the farmers' yield per acre. A journalist wrote that, "When Lord Woolton wants advice on the nutritional value of our wartime diet, he calls in first Dr. T. C. Drummond, a soft spoken unassuming man, scientific adviser to the Ministry of Food. His department acts as a clearing house for many ideas for improvements in food values that are brought before the Ministry by the nation's scientists (337)." Drummond and his assistants planned rations on a scientific basis.

Even the Ministry of Information had its scientists. In regulating the people's lives to such an extent, the government needed to know more about their attitudes and likely reactions. The Wartime Social Survey used the methods first introduced by Mass Observation and Gallup Poll in the late thirties; they were part of the now familiar sociological apparatus. The social sciences had arrived. Such methods enabled the government, and later private enterprise, to manipulate the public more easily. But the danger was not yet apparent. Most people were impressed by the new scientific strides. One man told a questioner: "I regard science as the one reliable thing in the world. I feel that science and its discoveries are the most thrilling thing in these times (338)."

This feeling became more ambivalent after the flying bombs and the dropping of the atomic bomb on the Japanese island, Hiroshima. The new weapons had to be weighed in the balance against the new drugs and technology, the vitamins and the fertilizers. For better or worse, scientists had responded to the demands of the war, and laid the basis for post-war technological Britain.

8 Rebuilding the Nation

The war turns

GENERAL MONTGOMERY's victory at El Alamein marked the turning point of the war in the West. At home, the desperate mood of the early months of 1942 vanished. Winston Churchill was cautiously optimistic: "This is not the end. It is not even the beginning of the end. But it is perhaps the end of the beginning (339)." A Member of Parliament commented that, "The changes in the news, the fact that success has displaced disaster and disappointment, that the army is coming into its own have all brought out added confidence in the people in the country. This has not prompted them to slacken their efforts in any way (340)."

Social disillusions

By 1943 there was a general feeling that the people deserved rewards for their valiant efforts of the past three years. The war had already made the government aware of distressing poverty in parts of the country. Welfare measures crept in slowly, not as the result of any socialist dogma, but in response to particular needs. The plight of the urban poor was brought into the open when slum children were sent to the country. One journal considered evacuation "the most important subject in the social history of the war, because it revealed to the whole people the black spots in its social life (341)." Women and children in the country were given better welfare services to dissuade them from returning to the towns.

During the blitz the poverty of the old people was noticed in the rest centres. The government introduced a new scheme for supplementary and unemployment pensions. As the *Times* said, "The proved need for supplementary pensions has been far greater than had been supposed, and the number of recipients will be about a million. There has therefore been a remarkable discovery of secret need ... The surprise is that for so many old people the level of existence should have been so low (342)."

Higher pensions, free milk under the National Milk Scheme of 1940, and school meals were given to people as their right, rather than as charitable relief. Trade Union leaders asked the government to apply the same principle to health insurance. The great advantage of the rich over the poor was their freedom from the fear of want in old age or ill health.

Beveridge Report William Beveridge, a former social worker and civil servant, was asked to draw up a comprehensive scheme extending this benefit to everybody. *The Beveridge Report* came out in December, 1942. It advocated "that organization of social insurance should be treated as one part only of a comprehensive policy of social progress. Social insurance fully developed may provide income security; it is an attack upon Want. But Want is one only of five giants on the road of reconstruction, and in some ways the easiest to attack. The others are Disease, Ignorance, Squalor and Idleness ... Social security must be achieved by co-operation between the state and the individual. The state should offer security for service and contribution (343)."

The public received the 200,000 word *Report* with extraordinary enthusiasm. The Stationery Office had a bestseller on its hands and long queues outside its doors. A social survey found that nineteen out of twenty people interviewed knew of the *Report*. It even featured on the most popular radio programme of all. Tommy Handley, posing as "His Fatuity, the Minister of Social Hilarity," told his listeners: "I've been up the last three days and nights reading the first chapter of a book called *Gone with the Want* by that stout fellow Beveridge (344)."

Charity or welfare? The government's reaction was less propitious. During the debate on the *Report*, Churchill claimed that the country was economically too weak to afford social insurance. "We must not forget that we are a Parliament in the eighth year and we have been justified in prolonging our existence only by the physical fact of the war situation ... We have no right whatever to tie the hands of future parliaments in regard to social matters which are their proper province (345)."

Harold Nicolson wrote to his wife complaining about "this form of charity, which will make people fold their arms and feel that they need have no enterprise, since everything will be provided for them (346)." A former Member of Parliament warned the Archbishop of Canterbury not to attend a meeting in support of the *Report*, because "every encroachment on individual liberty by the State should be regarded by Christians with suspicion, and not as necessarily good (347)." Such typical Tory attitudes infuriated Kingsley Martin who complained: "If we say that under the strain of war and the influence of bombing we are making important social strides, we are at once accused of the terrible crime of socialism (348)."

The debate on the *Report* hardened party attitudes. All members of the Labour Party who were not in the government pressed for its acceptance. The public remembered this in 1945, when it returned Labour to power. But Churchill put off its implementation. In February, 1943, a journalist commented that, "for all its fair words, the government lacks the courage either to accept or refuse the Beveridge plans (349)."

As the year passed an Allied victory seemed nearer. With the *Victories* capture of Tunis in May, 1943, General Montgomery and the American General Eisenhower completed the conquest of North Africa. Mussolini's capitulation was greeted with jubilation. Cecil Beaton "felt weak, and slightly tearful, but the others were just gay, smiling like children (350)." On *Itma's* hundredth programme, Sam Scramm announced, "Something wonderful's happened," and Tommy Handley replied: "I know. They've got a room ready for him in the Isle of Man (351)."

American help brought success in the Atlantic as well as North Africa and Italy. United States destroyers at last ended the U-boat menace. Thirty-seven U-boats were sunk in July alone, less shipping was lost, and imports began to rise once more. Germany's *Tirpitz* was damaged in September, and the *Scharnhorst* sunk in December. The Russians were sweeping the Germans back to their borders. The British queued for hours outside Westminster Abbey and in the Provinces to see the sword of Stalingrad, "made at the King's command as a gift to the steel-hearted people of Stalingrad . . . suffused with gratitude to their remote allies (352)."

Moreover, the sporadic raids had become almost bearable by *Optimism* now. When Harold Nicolson was walking "to the Green Park *at home* Underground, the siren went off. Nobody paid the slightest attention. It is a strange psychological fact that the sound of the siren gives one a sense almost of pleasure . . . Is it that we feel that

Survivors of the German battleship *Scharnhorst* are taken prisoner and blindfolded (December, 1943)

no serious raids are likely and that we enjoy being reminded of past dangers in present tranquillity? If and when raids begin again in earnest, then we shall have feelings of dread and fear (353)." They began again with the little blitz in January, 1944. Meanwhile, in September—according to a Mass Observation social survey—three out of four people believed that the war would be over within the year.

The general optimism was sometimes tempered with trepidation. George Orwell commented "on the strange fact, recently reported by the Mass Observers, and confirmed by my own limited experience, that many factory workers are actually afraid of the war ending, because they foresee a prompt return to the old conditions with three million unemployed (354)." Memories of the great depression lay at the back of everyone's mind. In one of his radio *Postscripts* J. B. Priestley had already reminded them "what we did for young men and their young wives at the end of the last war. We did nothing . . . After the cheering and the flag waving were over, and all the medals were given out, somehow the young heroes disappeared, but after a year or two there were a lot of shabby, young-oldish men about who didn't seem to have been lucky in the scramble for easy jobs and quick profits, and so tried to sell us second-hand cars or office supplies we didn't want (355)." The poet John Pudney voiced the same fears in *To Johnny, the pilot* (356):

> *Fetch out no shroud*
> *For Johnny in-the-cloud*
> *And keep your tears*
> *For him in after years.*
> *Better by far*
> *For Johnny-the-bright-star*
> *To keep your head*
> *And see his children fed.*

New society

As news of victories came in, people gave more thought to the future. Demands for "post-war planning" were heard. Many agreed with the pamphleteer who wrote: "It is not sufficient to say 'No' to the foul and horrid creed of Nazism. It is necessary to offer to the world an alternative to that creed. And what we offer must be something better than a return to the old democracy with its slums, its vast disparities of wealth, its acceptance of privilege, its injustice, cruelty and perpetual dangerous instability (357)." The same spirit inspired the allies to set up the United Nations Relief and Rehabilitation Administration in October, 1943. U.N.R.R.A. saved thousands of Europeans from starvation. It preceded the Allies' decision at the Yalta Conference in 1944 to go ahead with a United Nations Organization, and at San Francisco in 1945 to draft the United Nations Charter.

Meanwhile, at home, Churchill attacked the "war-aimers" who wanted to enlarge the purpose of the war beyond the enemy's defeat. He told the miners when they demanded nationalization: "Everything for the war, whether controversial or not, and nothing controversial that is not needed *bona fide* for the war (358)." Nevertheless, Churchill was forced to make concessions to the new demands. In March, he told the people over the radio that the government had a "duty to peer through the mists of the future to the end of the war (359)," and announced a four year plan of social measures. In November, he appointed Lord Woolton as Minister of Reconstruction with a seat in the War Cabinet.

The government's most important new measure was the Education Act. The President of the Board of Education was R. A. Butler, only thirty-eight years old. With other Tories like Quintin Hogg, Anthony Eden and Harold Macmillan he accepted —as much as the Labour leaders, Sir Stafford Cripps and Herbert Morrison—the need for state intervention in the organization of society. Before the war only fourteen per cent of all children went on from elementary to secondary schools; the rest left school at fourteen years' old. There were often as many as sixty children in a class. The closing of schools during the phoney war of 1939, and the damaging of many more during the blitz, had made the situation even worse. Butler's White Paper recommended the provision of secondary education for all in grammar, technical or secondary modern schools. The school leaving age was to be raised first to fifteen and then to sixteen years' old. When the proposals became law in January, 1944, a journalist commented: "Few measures have been so widely or so warmly welcomed as Mr. Butler's Education Bill (360)."

The church was compensated for losing control of its own schools by the introduction of compulsory prayers in every school every morning. The division of all children into three categories by examination was invidious. But the leaving age was raised to fifteen in 1947; and the vital achievement of the Act was the provision of some sort of secondary education for every child. Churchill called it "the greatest scheme of improved education that has ever been attempted by a responsible government (361)."

In the same broadcast Churchill promised: "Before this session is out we shall lay before you our proposals for the extension of national insurance (362)." The White Paper in September, 1944, accepted William Beveridge's idea of flat rate weekly payments and benefits. In November, the Ministry of National Insurance was set up; the following year family allowances were introduced for second and subsequent children.

Beveridge had demanded not only family allowances, but a reorganized health service as two essentials for his plan for social security. The first attempt at organizing the hospitals into any kind of coherent system had been Chamberlain's Emergency Hospital Service. This had been set up to deal with the expected air-raid casualties. The Director-General of the new Service pointed out that, "Prior to the repeated surveys, which have been made by the

Ministry of Health during the last eighteen months, there was little appreciation of the low standard of hospital accommodation in the country as a whole (363)." Poor people were not well cared for at home because doctors preferred to work in areas where they would get well paid. Researchers found that there were "proportionately seven times as many general practitioners in Kensington as in South Shields (364)."

The general health of the people improved during the war. One journalist's fear that, "In the air raid shelters of London . . . a severe epidemic of influenza or typhoid fever might soon have a death roll far in excess of that caused by bombs (365)," was unfounded. Epidemics of all kinds were kept to a minimum by the free vaccination of seven million children between 1940 and 1945. The rationing system ensured a healthy diet (see Chapter 5). The thousand doctors introduced into the factories under Bevin's direction helped to keep the workers physically fit. In these ways the state's intervention in health matters was to some extent accepted, even before Beveridge called for a reorganized health service.

The Minister of Health now introduced the White Paper on *A National Health Service*. It proposed: "To ensure that everybody in the country—irrespective of means, age, sex or occupation—shall have equal opportunity to benefit from the best and most up-to-date medical and allied services available . . . to provide the service free of charge (366)." Doctors under the scheme would become salaried servants of the state. Most of them joined in the general acclamation: "The first impression about the White Paper is that it is not only a skilful compromise on controversial issues, but a really progressive document (367)." Only the more prosperous doctors in control of the British Medical Association, who were led by their Secretary, the Radio Doctor, demanded that "nothing should be done to encourage the splitting of the medical profession into two groups (368)."

The Health Service had to wait until 1946 for the National Health Bill to become law. An attempt was made in June, 1944, to ensure Beveridge's third prerequisite for social security, the provision of full employment. Bevin's White Paper announced: "The Government accept as one of their primary aims and responsibilities the maintenance of a high and stable level of employment after the war (369)." The *Economist* considered the White Paper "a landmark in

*National
Health Act*

economic history . . . In the last half century there has been a steady encroachment of the state in the economic domain. But the process has been reluctant, hesitant . . . Now, for the first time there is a bold and conscious assumption of responsibility and authority over a whole vast terrain of policy (370)."

Housing problem
A journalist commented that the new White Paper "has had an amazingly tranquil reception (371)." The public were busier with such practical problems as where they were going to live. By the end of the war, more than two million houses were destroyed and five million made temporarily uninhabitable. No domestic building was allowed during the war years. In March, 1944, Churchill announced that, as well as reconstruction, "The second attack on the housing problem will be made by what are called the prefabricated or emergency houses . . . I hope we may make up to $1\frac{1}{2}$ million of these . . . They are superior to the ordinary cottage as it exists today: not only have they excellent baths, gas or electric kitchenettes and refrigerators; but their walls carry fitted furniture which today it would cost £80 to buy (372)." The public were delighted to see the small, box-like but comfortable, "pre-fabs" going up, even if only 160,000 of them materialized. They were only supposed to last ten years, but many are still in use today.

Social changes
Other visible signs of the end of the struggle were appearing. George Orwell noticed that "railings are returning in one London square after another." The government's moves in the direction of the welfare state did much to dampen the enthusiasm for social revolution, which some had feared and others hoped for in 1939. The only new Communist demonstrations were protests against Oswald Mosley's release. To George Orwell, the return of the iron railings was symbolic: "The lawful denizens of the squares can make use of their treasured keys again and the children of the poor can be kept out." He wanted clothes rationing retained because "since no real structural change is occurring in our society, the mechanical levelling process that results from sheer scarcity is better than nothing. If the poor are not much better dressed, at least the rich are shabbier (373)."

Clothes rationing remained, but trouser turn-ups reappeared. Hugh Dalton thought that men's morale had been depressed by insufficient pockets. He now told the House of Commons: "I have decided that men's suits may again be made without any restrictions on styles (374)." Pre-war sounds as well as sights were return-

One of the first prefabs (prefabricated houses) designed to fight the terrible housing shortage. Many still stand today

ing. Church bells were rung again, although as the columnist William Hickey pointed out, "There will be considerable practical difficulties in many places. Probably about half of the average village team of bellringers are young men now away in the forces or, which makes them equally unavailable on Sunday mornings, in the Home Guard (375)."

1944   In December, 1944, the position was improved when, as another sign of the times, the Home Guard was disbanded. The same month Civil Defence forces were released from their duties; there were even rumours that the boys from the front might also soon be home.

9 Victory

WINSTON CHURCHILL warned the English people over the radio in March, 1944: "This is not the time to talk about demobilization. The hour of our greatest effort and action is approaching . . . The flashing eyes of all our soldiers, sailors, and airmen must be fixed upon the enemy on their front. The only homeward road for all of us lies through the arch of victory (376)."

The second front was imminent. Churchill had been under pressure from President Roosevelt, at Washington in May and at Quebec in August, to set a date for Operation "Overlord," the European landing. At Teheran in November, Stalin had joined his voice to the President's. The Channel was safe from the U-boat menace. It was now accepted that aerial bombing alone would not defeat the Germans. France must be invaded by troops. To Sir Arthur Harris' disgust the bombing offensive was called off in April and bomber command placed under Eisenhower's supreme command of "Overlord." The devastation of Dresden the following February was Harris' last fling, but it was the responsibility of the government. After Dresden, both Harris and area bombing were discredited. *Operation Overlord*

Everybody knew that the invasion of Europe was coming, but nobody knew exactly when or where it would be launched. Convoys carried soldiers from their scattered camps to the South Coast. One diarist commented: "Our nights echoed to the ceaseless clatter of heavy tanks lumbering down the Bournemouth-Southampton road (377)." Thousands of skilled men were drafted to small, southern ports to make and assemble floating harbours. In spite of the numbers of people employed the secret was well kept.

Ed Murrow told his American listeners: " The planning of this operation is complex beyond description. Nothing like it has ever been seen. It is not just a matter of co-ordinating land, sea and air forces. It involves the loading of ships so that the things that are needed first will be the first to be unloaded. It means careful calculation of weather and tides . . . And it means security, thousands of people knowing small bits of the plan but only a very few having knowledge of how the whole thing fits together . . . As a matter of fact, there is less loose talk amongst civilians than ever before. It's as though everyone realized the importance of guarding the plans, even when most of the movements must be carried out within sight of the enemy's air reconnaissance (378)."

Diversion For the benefit of the enemy, mock landing craft were assembled on the East coast, in Kent and Essex. One writer saw the real preparations in Hampshire: "At every turn of every glade we found waggons and ammunition dumps, vainly sought by the Nazi observers, which the late-budding trees concealed (379)." Another journalist wrote on 26th May: "England is expectant, almost hushed. Every time we turn on the radio we expect to hear that the great invasion of Europe has begun . . . I know there are men and women who lie awake at night and cannot sleep for worry as to whether their sons will be "in it," and middle-aged men are sick that they should escape and their sons fall (380)."

D-Day D-Day came at last on 6th June, 1944. A B.B.C. newsreader announced the successful landings. In one land army hostel "that night was the first time that there was complete silence during the six o'clock news (381)." The following days were less quiet for anyone living near the coast. The flow of soldiers and equipment across the Channel continued. At his Kent home, Harold Nicolson wrote in his diary that the sky "is literally dominated by aeroplanes. All night they howl and rage above us. Then in daytime there is also much activity: great fleets of bombers floating slowly above us . . . And then the fighters at a lower level swishing along at enormous speeds. In London there is a continual crowd around the tickertape in the House of Commons corridor . . . The newspapers are snapped up the moment they appear on the streets . . . People are relieved that it has begun. They scan the weather a little more acutely than usual and notice the direction of the wind. But on the whole we are amazingly calm (382)."

The first The rejoicing and the calm were short lived. The following night
doodle-bug the first German flying bomb landed in Kent. Launched from bases

D-Day, 6th June, 1944. American and British ships carry armies over the
English Channel to Normandy, France, to defeat the Germans in Europe

in North West France, it was followed by 8,000 more during the
next six weeks. A writer described her first experience of the new
weapon: "At eleven the alert went and then the most extraordinary
thing happened. There came a noise that was quite new to us, like
a rattling of a quantity of chains . . . The rattling came, suddenly
stopped dead, and within a minute there was a violent explosion.
The smell of it was everywhere (383)."

There had been rumours in the previous Spring of unmanned
weapons. Churchill had warned everyone in his March broadcast
of "new forms of attack." But the doodle-bugs, as these flying
bombs came to be called, shocked and terrified the public. Kingsley
Martin described "a street in Central London from which a number
of respectably dressed and decorous citizens arise, dusting their
knees and eyeing each other a little dubiously. Then they burst out
laughing, 'That's the first time I've ever done that,' says one. 'Same
here' says another (384)." Freya Stark, the well-known travel
writer, felt that "one has gone back into the ages when men saw
the invisible take on a visible shape, and recognized their gods,
unreasonable in human ways, full of fascination and terror (385)."

107

The terror was certainly visible. Harold Nicolson described how, "By day . . . one can see its little black body hurtling along with something flapping behind it which looks like gauze being blown out from an electric fan, but which is really the exhaust. At night this exhaust flames like a meteor, and one can follow the thing as it hurtles through the sky like a falling star, like a moving beacon, tense, deliberate, unswerving, vindictive, horribly purposeful (386)."

Rocket threat

The flying bomb killed over 6,000 people, most of whom were Londoners. By the end of July anti-aircraft measures were preventing all but one in seven getting through. But in September, "There was a loud explosion in London at dawn. It is the V2, (387)" wrote Nicolson. The new rockets took nearly 3,000 lives. The menace was defeated before the end of the year by the capture of their launching pads in northern France and Holland. In August, 1944, the Allies had landed in Southern France and marched North to take Paris. But despite this advance, and despite the fall of Rome in June which had passed almost unnoticed in the excitement of D-Day, the mood of the people had changed since the optimistic months of late 1943. The "little blitz" of January and February had "created far more fear than the great blitz of

1940-41. People dreaded another Winter of war (388)," wrote Nicolson. The flying bombs and rockets had a far worse effect on morale. Kingsley Martin also pointed out the contrast with the blitz; "In 1940, London believed that it was in the front line . . . Everywhere men and women were braced to endure, to organize and to carry on. In 1944 . . . we have been induced to believe that the war is over . . . People feel they 'have had it' (389)."

Personal losses were no longer quite so bravely borne. Yet in France, and in the Far East, as many men were actually fighting as at any time during the war. The scene in *English Family*, a contemporary novel, was still played horribly frequently: "This was the tenth day after D-Day, a gusty day with a grey sky . . . They were having lunch when the telephone rang. The voice at the other end was faint, almost disembodied. It said 'There's a telegram.' 'Who from?' 'War Office—It's about David' (390)."

Then, in December, the German offensive in the Ardennes caused more casualties. Many people were humiliated by the government's decision to intervene against the Communist resistance forces in the Greek civil war. By the end of the month Kingsley Martin thought "people less anxious to maintain the convention of jollification than in previous war Christmases." The hope was strong that the main fighting would be over in Europe and that the men would be coming home from the front. The disappointing fact that the Germans could still stage such a ferocious come-back was cruel, and the thought of the ghastly fighting in Belgium never out of anyone's mind. Added to the bitterness was the moral bewilderment and, in many cases, a sense of shame about Greece. "An airman I picked up on the road said: 'We are all confused about Greece. We know it can't be right that we should be fighting people who have just been fighting the Germans with us' (391)." *German comeback*

But the Ardennes offensive was Hitler's last throw. By diverting his troops from the east he gave the Russians their opportunity. By February they were within forty miles of Berlin. In March, both the Americans and the British crossed the Rhine. In April, Alexander completed the conquest of nothern Italy. In three consecutive days Mussolini was shot, the Germans in Italy surrendered and Hitler and his mistress committed suicide. On 7th May, 1945, at Rheims, General Eisenhower accepted the Germans' unconditional surrender. *Capitulation*

"The evil-doers now lie prostrate before us," Churchill told the people the following day, when Victory in Europe was celebrated. His broadcast was relayed over loudspeakers to the crowds outside the Houses of Parliament. "They've been streaming towards Buckingham Palace, the Houses of Parliament, Trafalgar Square and Piccadilly," Ed Murrow told his listeners, and, "As you walk down the street you hear singing that comes from open windows . . . Many women are wearing flags in their hats; some are even draped in flags. At times, someone will start to shout. There's no reason for the shout, but it's taken up at once . . . The scars of war are all about. There is no lack of serious, solemn faces. Their minds must be filled with memories of friends who died in the streets where they now walk, and of others who died from Burma to the Elbe (392)."

Despite the serious faces, there was wild excitement for one day. The Mall was a solid mass of people linking arms and singing. A journalist wrote: "In one crowded, crazy day, in one small patch of London, I've been passionately kissed by three girls . . . I've sung *Land of Hope and Glory* till I'm hoarse . . . I've climbed my first and positively my last lamp-post, and I've nearly persuaded myself, but not quite, that the war is over . . . Peace is something you need time to get used to. On the night of VE day, it still looked wrong to see naked lights blazing through the windows (393)."

Demobs   Many people returned that night to patched or temporary homes. They could switch on the lights but they could hardly end their victory celebrations with a feast. The ration of bacon and lard had been reduced only that month. Many who were demobbed from the forces had the added stress of returning as strangers to their wives and families and finding work for themselves. On 16th May, Bevin announced his plans for demobilization. First to be returned home would be the priority workers, such as the builders, and the rest would come according to a scrupulously fair calculation of age and length of service. It worked well. The 380 dispersal centres ejected a flow of men carrying their "demob suit," shirt, two collars, two pairs of socks, one pair of shoes, a tie, a hat and a "resettlement" booklet—all in a large flat box. But the flow never became a flood to inundate the labour market.

Politics   While the city streets filled up that Spring with more and more young men in their demob suits, posters of a tin-hatted private were plastered on the walls. Underneath was the caption, "This is your chance to *Labour* for him. Vote Labour and win the peace."

Left Crowds line London's streets to celebrate Victory in Europe on VE-Day (May, 1945). *Right* The Labour Party leader, Clement Attlee, campaigns against Churchill in the 1945 general election.

There had been no election since 1935. During the war Parliament had been prolonged annually. The Labour Party now insisted on an immediate election. Many people agreed with one writer who felt: "Surely Churchill, hero of all the world, whom even the people of Berlin clapped when he strode through their bomb-pitted streets, could not fail to be chosen by his own country? (394)."

Gratitude was not in question; but it was not enough. As one correspondent put it: "I think him quite the wrong man for directing the reconstruction of England. Our debt to him is probably greater than to any other politician in our history, but I could not feel on that account any obligation to vote for him (395)."

During the war many people had become aware of, and involved in, political activity who had previously considered such things to be none of their business. A journalist commented during the blitz that the shelter committees "are recruited mainly from people who have never found any kind of expression hitherto in active political or administrative work—the back street acquiescents. Now they are suddenly finding self-expression and self-confidence (396)."

The Army Bureau of Current Affairs kept the forces fully informed about politics, organizing debates and discussion groups. Civilians and soldiers between them bought a quarter of a million copies of *Guilty Men* and 600,000 copies of the *Beveridge Report*. The first pointed out that it was the Tory diehards of the pre-war National Government who had been responsible for the three unforgiveable sins: the dole, unemployment and appeasement. The parliamentary vote on the second convinced them that it was the Labour Party which really cared about their security and welfare.

Labour   The Labour Party's record in the debates on education, the health service and unemployment was a good one. A Gallup Poll taken in June, 1945, found that four out of ten people still thought the housing problem even more important than these issues. They had faith in Bevin's sincerity when he told them, "The better the house, the better people . . . New gardens and a new environment will make an enormous difference (397)." And they believed him when, at a meeting at Brentford, he promised them over four million new houses.

The Labour Party manifesto, *Let Us Face the Future,* promised the people the sort of society they had come to demand, including nationalization of many industries. The war not only proved that the Labour Party, by its participation in the coalition, was again fit to govern. It had also accustomed everyone to the idea of government handling the economy. The people didn't much like Churchill's party political broadcast: "I declare to you from the bottom of my heart that no socialist system can be established without a political police (398)." Nor was his attack on the chairman of the Labour Party, Harold Laski, as the head of a future British Gestapo very creditable. Moreover, the Conservatives' manifesto had little positive to offer the electorate. Churchill himself told his doctor: "I am worried about this damned election. I have no message for them now (399)."

Churchill out,   The electorate went to the polls on 5th July, 1945. When their
Attlee in   ballot slips were counted ten days later, after the forces' postal votes had come in, it was found that they had given the Labour

112   Party its first ever working majority. It won 393 seats to the Con-

In 1945 Winston Churchill retained his own seat here at Woodford, Essex,
but lost the general election

servatives' 213, the Liberals' 12 and the Independents' 22. Clement Attlee had attended the first session of the Potsdam conference with Churchill. He now returned as Prime Minister, accompanied by his Foreign Secretary, Ernest Bevin, to continue discussions with the Allied powers. Churchill had already given formal consent to the use of the atomic bomb. The first was dropped on Hiroshima on 6th August, 1945. John Lehmann recorded in his journal the most typical reaction at home: "The explosion of the atom bomb over Japan has made me physically sick (400)." On the 9th August the second bomb was dropped on Nagasaki. On the 14th August the Japanese surrendered.

Britain's war
debts
The swift and unexpected armistice increased Britain's economic plight. For the end of the war meant, under Harry Truman—President since Roosevelt's death in April—the end of American Lend-Lease. Britain's external debts had increased to £3,000,000,000. She had lost a third of her shipping. Even more tragic and just as vital to her economy, she had lost 300,000 men in the armed forces and 60,000 civilians in air raids. Lord Keynes told the new Cabinet that Britain faced "without exaggeration and without implying that we should not recover from it, a financial Dunkirk (401)." Shortages, controls and rationing continued. The allocation of clothing coupons was again cut in September, and bread rationing was yet to follow. But if the economic struggle continued at least the people's war was over.

Churchill's
message
After the news of his electoral defeat, Churchill thanked the British people for making possible the more important victory in war: "I have laid down the charge which was placed upon me in darker times . . . It only remains for me to express to the British people for whom I have acted in these perilous years my profound gratitude for their unflinching unswerving support which they have given me during my task (402)."

When his doctor mentioned the people's ingratitude, he replied, "Oh no, I wouldn't call it that. They have had a very hard time (403)."

Further Reading

SEVERAL OFFICIAL HISTORIES, based on government papers, give a sound detailed account of war-time Britain. The most interesting and best written is R.M. Titmuss, *Problems of Social Policy* (H.M.S.O. & Longmans, London, 1950; Longmans, New York, 1950). Also very helpful are W.K. Hancock and M. Gowing, *British War Economy* (H.M.S.O., London, 1949); R. S. Sayers, *Financial Policy* (H.M.S.O., London, 1956); and M. M. Postan, *British War Production* (H.M.S.O., London, 1952). Winston Churchill's *The Second World War* (Cassell, London, 1948; Houghton Mifflin, Boston, 1948) in six splendid volumes, is also based on contemporary records but is naturally both more concerned with overall strategy and more personally biased. The best background work is A. J. P. Taylor's *English History 1914-45*, Volume XV of the *Oxford History of England* (O.U.P. London and New York, 1965). A recent book, Angus Calder's *The People's War* (Cape, London, 1969; Pantheon Books, New York, 1969) covers the social aspects in detail. E. S. Turner's *The Phoney War on the Home Front* (Michael Joseph, London, 1962; St. Martin's Press, New York, 1962) is less ambitious but just as entertaining.

Two aspects of the struggle at home are well described by Charles Graves in *The Home Guard of Britain* (Hutchinson, London, 1943) and *Women in Green: The Story of the W.V.S.* (Heinemann, London, 1948). Basil Dean's *Theatre at War* (Harrap, London, 1956; Clarke Irwin, New York, 1957) and Asa Briggs' *The War of Words* (O.U.P., London 1970), the third volume in his *History of Broadcasting in the United Kingdom* are both invaluable. C. P. Snow's *Science and Government* (O.U.P., London, 1960; New American Library, New York) is a fascinating account of the Lindemann-Tizard conflict. Of the two biographies of Lindemann, *The Professor in Two Worlds* by Lord Birkenhead is the official life (Collins, London, 1961; Houghton Mifflin, Boston, 1962) and *The Prof* by Roy Harrod (Macmillan, London, 1959; Macmillan, New York, 1959) more personal.

Alan Bullock's *Ernest Bevin*, volume II, is the most useful and also very readable relevant biography (Heinemann, London, 1960). Sir J. W.

116

Wheeler-Bennett has written the lives of both *Sir John Anderson* (Macmillan, London, 1962; St. Martin's Press, New York, 1963) and *King George VI* (Macmillan, London, 1958; St. Martin's Press, New York, 1958). Other intriguing biographies are Ted Kavanagh's *Tommy Handley* (Hodder & Stoughton, London, 1949) and J. A. Cole's *Lord Haw-Haw* (Faber, London, 1964; Farrar, Straus, New York, 1965).

The Mass Observation reports prepared by Tom Harrisson and Charles Madge describe and quote contemporary attitudes. Some of these attitudes are superbly portrayed in Evelyn Waugh's post-war trilogy, *Men at Arms* (Penguin, London and Baltimore, 1970), *Officers and Gentlemen* (Penguin, London and Baltimore, 1970), and *Unconditional Surrender* (Penguin, London and Baltimore, 1970). None of the war-time novels of Graham Greene, Joyce Cary or J. B. Priestley deal directly with the war, but all shed incidental light on life during these years.

The best general pictorial records of war-time Britain are perhaps Bill Brandt's photographs; and the most pungent comments on both the government and the people are David Low's cartoons, collected in *Years of Wrath* (Gollancz, London, 1949; Simon & Schuster, New York, 1946).

Table of Events

1938

September 29th Neville Chamberlain meets Adolf Hitler at Munich

1939

May 8th Conscription of twenty and twenty-one year old men
August 22nd Nazi-Soviet Pact
August 24th Emergency Powers (Defence) Act
September 3rd Declaration of war with Germany
National Service (Armed Forces) Act extends conscription
October 14th *Royal Oak* sunk at Scapa Flow

1940

April 9th Hitler invades Norway and Denmark
May 9th Neville Chamberlain resigns and Winston Churchill becomes Prime Minister
May 13th Ernest Bevin becomes Minister of Labour and National Service
May 14th L.D.V. (Home Guard) formed
May 22nd Emergency Powers (Defence) Act extended
May 26th Retreat from Dunkirk

June 17th   Fall of France
August 8th   Battle of Britain begins
September 7th   German night raids on London begin
November 14th   German air raid on Coventry

1941

January 12th   People's Convention meeting
January 21st   *Daily Worker* newspaper closed down
March 5th   Essential Work Orders introduced
March 11th   Lend-Lease Act
March 20th   Plymouth bombed
April 6th   Allied forces expelled from Greece
April 7th   Kingsley Wood's budget extends Income Tax
May 10th   Rudolph Hess lands in Scotland
June 22nd   Hitler attacks Russia
September 22nd   "Tanks for Russia" week begins
December 2nd   Conscription of women announced
December 7th   Japanese attack Pearl Harbour
December 10th   *Prince of Wales* and *Repulse* sunk

1942

February 4th   Winston Churchill reconstitutes Cabinet
February 12th   *Scharnhorst* and *Gneisenau* sail through Channel
February 15th   Fall of Singapore
February 23rd   Sir Arthur Harris becomes Chief of Bomber
                   Command
March 19th   *Daily Mirror* warns against subversion
April 14th   *Baedeker* raids begin
July 1st   Censure motion on Churchill after fall of Tobruk
August 19th   Abortive Dieppe landing
November 4th   Montgomery wins Battle of El Alamein in North
                   Africa
November 22nd   Battle of Stalingrad
December 1st   Beveridge Report published

1943

January 14th	Churchill meets President Roosevelt at Casablanca
May 7th	Montgomery captures Tunis (North Africa)
July 9th	Allied invasion of Sicily
September 3rd	Italy surrenders
December 2nd	Balloting for "Bevin boys" introduced
December 26th	*Scharnhorst* sunk in Battle of North Cape

1944

January 14th	R. A. Butler introduces Education Act
January 21st	"Little Blitz" begins
January 22nd	Allied landings at Anzio (Italy)
June 4th	Fall of Rome
June 6th	D-Day
June 9th	White Paper on Employment Policy
June 12th	First flying bomb
August 25th	Fall of Paris
September 8th	First rocket falls on London
December 3rd	Home Guard disbanded
December 19th	Civil Defence forces disbanded

1945

February 14th	British bomber raids on Dresden
April 12th	Death of President Roosevelt
May 7th	Germany surrenders
May 8th	V.E. (Victory in Europe) Day
July 5th	Polling day in Britain
July 17th	Potsdam Conference
August 6th	Atomic bomb dropped on Hiroshima, Japan
August 14th	Japan surrenders

Notes on Sources

(1) Draft article for *The Record* (7th February, 1938)
(2) George Orwell, *The Lion and the Unicorn* (1941)
(3) Margery Allingham, *The Oaken Heart* (1941)
(4) Mass Observation, *War Begins at Home* (Survey, 12th September, 1939)
(5) Mass Observation, *Britain* (Interview, 22nd September, 1938)
(6) *Star* (22nd September, 1938)
(7) *Times* (26th September, 1938)
(8) Broadcast (27th September, 1938)
(9) Louis MacNeice, *Autumn Journal* (March, 1939)
(10) Margery Allingham, *The Oaken Heart* (1941)
(11) *Times* (4th October, 1938)
(12) Air Staff Report, quoted R. M. Titmuss, *Problems of Social Policy* (1950)
(13) Basil Liddell-Hart *The Defence of Britain* (1939)
(14) Ministry of Health circular (24th July, 1939)
(15) Henry Green, *Caught* (1942)
(16) Margery Allingham, *The Oaken Heart* (1941)
(17) Mass Observation, *Britain* (1939)
(18) Mass Observation, *War Begins at Home* (1940)
(19) Broadcast (2nd July, 1939)
(20) Official leaflet, quoted Mass Observation, *War Begins at Home*
(21) Chamberlain letter to George VI (23rd August, 1939)
(22) Mass Observation, *War Begins at Home* (Interview, 26th August, 1939)
(23) W. Churchill, *The Gathering Storm* (1948)
(24) *The Outbreak of War*, H.M.S.O. (1939)
(25) The Ironside Diaries (3rd September, 1939)
(26) Cecil Beaton, *The Years Between* (3rd December, 1939)
(27) Mass Observation, *War Begins at Home* (14th October, 1939)
(28) Verily Anderson, *Spam Tomorrow* (1956)
(29) Henry Green, *Caught*
(30) J. L. Hodson, *Before Daybreak* (1941)
(31) Ed Murrow, *This is London* broadcast (15th October, 1939)
(32) Joyce Cary, *Charley is My Darling* (1946)
(33) John Lehmann, *I am My Brother* (1960)
(34) A. P. Herbert, *Sunday Graphic,* "Siren Song" (10th March, 1940)
(35) Evelyn Waugh, *Put Out More Flags* (1942)
(36) *Hansard* (8th May, 1939)
(37) Ed Murrow, *In Search of Light* broadcast (31st August, 1939)
(38) Evelyn Waugh, *Put Out More Flags* (1942)
(39) *Evening Standard* (2nd January, 1940)
(40) Harold Nicolson letter to Vita Sackville West (4th June, 1940)
(41) Ralph Ingersoll, *Report on England* (1941)
(42) *Woman's Own* (18th September, 1942)
(43) *New Statesman,* London Diary (28th August, 1943)
(44) Anthony Weymouth, *Plague Year* (31st March, 1940)
(45) Fenner Brockway, *Outside the Right* (1963)
(46) Evelyn Waugh, *Men at Arms* (1952)
(47) *Daily Express* (1st September, 1939)
(48) *North London Collegiate School Magazine* (December, 1939) quoted Asa Briggs, *They Saw it Happen*
(49) Bernard Kops, *The World is a Wedding* (1963)
(50) Richard Pedley, *Evacuation Survey* (1940)
(51) National Federation of Women's Institutes: A survey of evacuation (1940)
(52) Bernard Kops, *The World is a Wedding*
(53) N.F.W.I. evacuation survey
(54) C. McCall, *Women's Institutes* (1943)
(55) Bernard Kops, *The World is a Wedding*
(56) Margery Allingham, *The Oaken Heart*
(57) Harold Nicolson, *Diaries and Letters* (Entry 14th September, 1939)
(58) N.F.W.I. evacuation survey
(59) Joyce Cary, *Charley is My Darling* (1946)
(60) *New Statesman,* London Diary (23rd September, 1939)
(61) Maurice Edelman,

Production for Victory
(1941)

(62) Vera Brittain, *England's Hour* (1941)

(63) *Hansard* (9th October, 1940)

(64) Mass Observation, *War Begins at Home* (Interview, November, 1939)

(65) Verily Anderson, *Spam Tomorrow* (1956)

(66) *Times* (2nd November, 1939)

(67) Vera Brittain, *England's Hour* (November, 1941)

(68) J. L. Hodson, *Through the Dark Night* (Entry 6th January, 1940)

(69) John Lehmann, *I am My Brother*

(70) Evelyn Waugh, *Men at Arms*

(71) *Daily Herald* (12th September, 1939) .

(72) Kingsley Wood to Leo Amery, quoted Leo Amery, *My Political Life*, vol *iii*

(73) Cato, *Guilty Men* (May, 1940)

(74) Chamberlain's speech to Central Council of National Union of Conservative and Unionist Associations (5th April, 1940)

(75) *Daily Mail* (10th May, 1940)

(76) Leo Amery, *Hansard* (7th May, 1940)

(77) Winston Churchill, *The Gathering Storm*

(78) Mass Observation, *War Begins at Home*

(79) John Lehmann, *I am My Brother*

(80) J. B. Priestley, *Postscript* broadcast (7th July, 1940)

(81) Winston Churchill, *The Gathering Storm*

(82) Harold Nicolson, *Diaries and Letters* (Entry 9th September, 1941)

(83) *Hansard* (13th May, 1940)

(84) Margery Allingham, *The Oaken Heart*

(85) Harold Nicolson to Vita Sackville West (26th May, 1940)

(86) Harold Nicolson, *Diaries and Letters* (Entry 25th May, 1940)

(87) J. B. Priestley, *Postscript* broadcast (5th June, 1940)

(88) Harold Nicolson, *Diaries and Letters* (Entry 1st June, 1940)

(89) *Hansard* (4th June, 1940)

(90) *Hansard* (18th June, 1940)

(91) George VI to Queen Mary (27th June, 1940)

(92) *New Statesman*, London Diary (1st June, 1940)

(93) *Times* (11th July, 1940)

(94) *Time and Tide* (22nd June, 1940) letter from George Orwell

(95) *Partisan Review* (August, 1941), George Orwell's "London Letter"

(96) J. B. Priestley, *Postscript* broadcast (16th June, 1940)

(97) Charles Graves, *Londoner's Life* (13th March, 1942)

(98) *Ibid* (10th January, 1942)

(99) *Partisan Review* (August, 1941), George Orwell's "London Letter"

(100) Evelyn Waugh, *Put Out More Flags*

(101) J. B. Priestley, *Postscript* broadcast (14th July, 1940)

(102) Ernest Bevin, *The Job to be Done* (1942)

(103) *Daily Mail* (23rd May, 1940)

(104) *Ibid* (24th May, 1940)

(105) Bishop Bell, *Humanity and the Refugees*, Lucien Woolf Memorial lecture (1st February, 1939)

(106) J. B. Priestley, *Blackout in Gretley* (1942)

(107) *Daily Mail* (24th May, 1940)

(108) Ed Murrow, *In Search of Light* broadcast (30th May, 1940)

(109) *Hansard* (22nd August, 1940)

(110) Ralph Ingersoll, *Report on England*

(111) *Ibid*

(112) *Daily Mail* (24th May, 1940)

(113) Claud Cockburn, *Crossing the Line* (1958)

(114) Margery Allingham, *The Oaken Heart*

(115) Evelyn Waugh, *Men at Arms*

(116) Jonah Barrington, *Daily Express* (14th September, 1939)

(117) Cassandra, *Daily Mirror* (25th September, 1939)

(118) Hannen Swaffer, *Worlds Press News* (2nd February, 1940)

(119) *New Statesman*, London Diary (8th June, 1940)

(120) A. P. Herbert, *Sunday Graphic* (19th May, 1940); "Rumours"

(121) J. B. Priestley, *Postscript* broadcast (23rd June, 1940)

(122) *Ibid* (21st July, 1940)

(123) George Orwell, *Wartime Diary* (Entry 21st October, 1940)

(124) *Times* (8th November, 1939)

(125) Ralph Ingersoll, *Report on England*

(126) Maurice Edelman, *Production for Victory*

(127) J. B. Priestley, *Postscript* broadcast (6th October, 1940)

(128) *Manchester Guardian* (9th July, 1940)

(129) J. L. Hodson, *Through the Dark Night* (Entry 3rd April, 1940)

(130) *Partisan Review* (March, 1941), George Orwell's "London Letter"

(131) *Times* (1st July, 1940)

(132) Ursula Bloom, *War isn't Wonderful* (Entry, 25th April, 1940)

(133) A. P. Herbert, *Sunday Graphic* (April, 1940), "The Devil to Pay"

(134) *Daily Mirror* (10th July, 1940)

(135) *Hansard* (1st December, 1942)

(136) *Woman's Own* (31st May, 1941)

(137) *Times* (27th August, 1940)

(138) *Daily Mirror* (3rd August, 1940)

(139) *Ibid* (19th August, 1940)

(140) Marcel Jullian, *The Battle of Britain* (1967)

(141) Ed Murrow, "In Search of Light" broadcast (8th September, 1940)

(142) A. P. Herbert, *The Thames* (1966)

(143) Ralph Ingersoll, *Report on England*

(144) *Hansard* (20th August, 1940)

(145) Anthony Weymouth, *Plague Year* (Entry 11th October, 1940)

(146) Ralph Ingersoll, *Report on England*

(147) Harold Nicolson, *Diaries and Letters* (Entry 19th September, 1940)

(148) Graham Greene, *The Ministry of Fear* (1943)

(149) T. S. Eliot, *Four Quartets—Little Gidding*

(150) *New Statesman*, London Diary (28th September, 1940)

(151) *Daily Express* (1st October, 1940)

(152) Harold Nicolson, *Diaries and Letters* (Entry 16th May, 1941)

(153) Verily Anderson, *Spam Tomorrow*

(154) Vera Brittain, *England's Hour*

(155) Dylan Thomas, *A Refusal to Mourn the Death, by Fire, of a Child in London*

(156) Ralph Ingersoll, *Report on England*

(157) *Ibid*

(158) J. L. Hodson, *Through the Dark Night* (Entry 2nd October, 1940)

(159) Mark Benny, *Over to Bombers* (1943)

(160) J. B. Priestley, *Postscript* broadcast (22nd September, 1940)

(161) Ralph Ingersoll, *Report on England*

(162) *Ibid*

(163) Broadcast (11th September, 1940)

(164) Ed Murrow, broadcast (18th September, 1940)

(165) John Winant, letter from Grosvenor Square (Entry April, 1941)

(166) King's Diary (18th November, 1940), quoted Wheeler-Bennett, *George VI*

(167) J. L. Hodson, *Towards the Morning* (Entry 9th February, 1941)

(168) Harold Nicolson, *Diaries and Letters* (Entry 7th May, 1941)

(169) *Times* (18th September, 1941)

(170) J. L. Hodson, *Towards the Morning* (Entry 9th February, 1941)

(171) *Daily Express* (1st October, 1940)

(172) Ralph Ingersoll, *Report on England*

(173) Broadcast to Australia (17th February, 1941)

(174) Harold Nicolson, *Diaries and Letters* (Entry 21st September, 1943)

(175) *Times* (26th September, 1938)

(176) Bernard Kops, *The World is a Wedding*

(177) *Ibid*

(178) Ralph Ingersoll, *Report on England*

(179) *Daily Express* (1st October, 1940)

(180) *Daily Express* (11th October)

(181) Ritchie Calder, *New Statesman* (8th March, 1941)

(182) Graham Greene, *Ministry of Fear*

(183) *Evening News* (9th October, 1940)

(184) *Hansard* (9th October, 1940)

(185) Charity Organization Society Report to R. M. Titmuss (September, 1943)

(186) *Daily Express* (1st October, 1940

(187) Cabinet Paper, (September, 1941)

(188) George Orwell, *The Lion and the Unicorn* (1941)

(189) Harold Nicolson, *Diaries and Letters* (Entry 17th September, 1940)

(190) *Partisan Review* (March, 1941), George Orwell's "London Letter"

(191) *New Statesman*, London Diary (8th March, 1941)

(192) J. L. Hodson, *Towards the Morning* (Entry 6th February, 1941)

(193) Claud Cockburn, *Crossing the Line*

(194) J. B. Priestley, *Blackout in Gretley*

(195) *Partisan Review* (August, 1941), George Orwell's "London Letter"

(196) Beaverbrook speech (22nd September, 1941), quoted Kenneth Young, *Churchill and Beaverbrook* (1967)

(197) Evelyn Waugh, *Officers and Gentlemen* (1955)

123

(198) *Times* (27th December, 1940)

(199) J. L. Hodson, *Towards the Morning* (Entry 3rd April, 1940)

(200) *Times* (15th September, 1941)

(201) Ralph Ingersoll, *Report on England*

(202) *Times* (14th November, 1939)

(203) *Ibid*

(204) *Times* (15th November, 1939)

(205) *Ibid*

(206) Charles Madge, *War Time Pattern of Saving and Spending* (1943)

(207) J. L. Hodson, *Before Daybreak* (Entry 29th May 1941)

(208) *News Chronicle* (14th July, 1941)

(209) Lend-Lease Act (11th March, 1941)

(210) Harold Nicolson, *Diaries and Letters* (Entry 21st March, 1941)

(211) Ed Murrow, *In Search of Light* broadcast (9th March, 1941)

(212) Harold Nicolson, *Diaries and Letters* (Entry 10th December, 1941)

(213) *Hansard* (27th January, 1942)

(214) J. B. Priestley, *Blackout in Gretley*

(215) George VI letter to Queen Mary (16th February, 1942), quoted Wheeler-Bennett, *George VI*

(216) Verily Anderson, *Spam Tomorrow*

(217) Broadcast (15th February, 1942)

(218) *Hansard* (25th February, 1942)

(219) Churchill minute to Lindemann (5th March, 1942)

(220) J. L. Hodson, *English Family* (1947)

(221) *Partisan Review* (August 1942), George Orwell's "London Letter"

(222) *Bristol Evening Post* (20th January, 1943)

(223) Graham Greene, *The Ministry of Fear*

(224) A. P. Herbert, *Let Us be Glum—Ode to an Egg* (1942)

(225) Charles Graves, *Londoner's Life* (Entry 10th January, 1942)

(226) Ralph Ingersoll, *Report on England* (Entry 4th August, 1943)

(227) Charles Graves, *Londoner's Life* (Entry 14th March, 1942)

(228) *Partisan Review* (July, 1943) George Orwell's "London Letter"

(229) J. L. Hodson *English Family*

(230) *Partisan Review* (November 1942), George Orwell's "London Letter"

(231) Verily Anderson, *Spam Tomorrow*

(232) *Daily Mirror* (16th March, 1942)

(233) Ursula Bloom, *War isn't Wonderful* (Entry 10th January, 1943)

(234) Ed Murrow, broadcast (16th May, 1943)

(235) *Daily Express* (14th September, 1939)

(236) Ralph Ingersoll, *Report on England*

(237) Hugh Dalton letter to William Temple (30th August, 1942)

(238) Mass Observation, *Puzzled People* (1947)

(239) J. L. Hodson, *The Sea and the Land* (Entry 29th August, 1943)

(240) *Tribune* (3rd December, 1943)

(241) *Partisan Review* (March, 1943), George Orwell's "London Letter"

(242) *Daily Express* (26th September, 1941)

(243) *Daily Mirror* (12th March, 1942)

(244) J. B. Priestley, *Blackout in Gretley*

(245) *News Chronicle* (28th March, 1942)

(246) *Daily Mirror* (13th March, 1942)

(247) King's Diary (30th April, 1942), quoted Wheeler-Bennett, *George VI*

(248) *Times* (8th September, 1941)

(249) *Partisan Review* (July, 1942), George Orwell's "London Letter"

(250) Harold Nicolson, *Diaries and Letters* (Entry 22nd June, 1942)

(251) *Evening News* (11th October, 1939)

(252) *Times* (14th November, 1939)

(253) J. M. Keynes, *How to Pay for the War* (1940)

(254) *Hansard* (21st January, 1941)

(255) *New Statesman* (8th March, 1941)

(256) J. L. Hodson, *Through the Dark Night* (Entry 3rd April, 1940)

(257) King's Diary (3rd March, 1940), quoted Wheeler-Bennett, *George VI*

(258) *Economist* (7th December, 1940)

(259) Emergency Powers Defence Bill (22nd May, 1940)

(260) Broadcast to Australia (17th February, 1941)

(261) *Daily Mail* (15th May, 1940)

(262) J. T. Murphy, *Victory Production* (1942)

(263) *Woman's Own* (24th July, 1942)

(264) Mass Observation, *People in Production* (1942)

(265) Ernest Bevin letter to John Winant, quoted Alan Bullock *Ernest Bevin* (1960)

(266) *News Chronicle* (22nd May, 1942)

(267) *Hansard* (2nd April, 1941)
(268) Mass Observation, People in Production
(269) *Hansard* (29th July, 1941)
(270) Ernest Bevin speech to mass meeting at Liverpool (28th June, 1942)
(271) J. B. Pick, *Under the Crust* (1946)
(272) R. Page-Arnot, *The Miners in Crisis and War* (1961)
(273) *Hansard* (7th May, 1942)
(274) *Hansard* (2nd December, 1943)
(275) J. B. Pick, *Under the Crust* (1946)
(276) *Times* (23rd December, 1940)
(277) Victoria Sackville-West, *The Women's Land Army* (1944)
(278) *Daily Mirror* (6th July, 1940)
(279) Evelyn Waugh, *Men at Arms*
(280) *Times* (1st July, 1940)
(281) J. L. Hodson, *Towards the Morning* (Entry 14th March, 1941)
(282) *Times* (1st July, 1940)
(283) C. S. Orwin, *Speed the Plough* (1942)
(284) Farmers' Rights Association, *Living Casualties* (1950)
(285) *Ibid*
(286) *Times* (11th October, 1940)
(287) Ernest Bevin, *The Job to be Done*
(288) *I.T.M.A* broadcast 19th September, 1939)
(289) Evelyn Waugh, *Men at Arms*
(290) J. L. Hodson, *Towards the Morning* (Entry 7th January, 1941)
(291) *Times* (19th August, 1940)
(292) *Times* (30th August, 1940)
(293) J. L. Hodson, *The Sea and the Land* (Entry 5th August, 1943)
(294) *Partisan Review* (Spring 1944), George Orwell's "London Letter"
(295) Ed Murrow, *In Search of Light* broadcast (30th May, 1940)
(296) *Daily Mirror* (20th March 1942)
(297) Charles Graves, *Londoner's Life* (Entries 2nd April and 31st March, 1942)
(298) Harold Nicolson, *Diaries and Letters* (Entry 8th October 1942)
(299) Evelyn Waugh, *Officers and Gentlemen*
(300) *Partisan Review* (March, 1941), George Orwell's "London Letter"
(301) Charles Graves, *Londoner's Life* (Entry 2nd April, 1942)
(302) Vera Brittain, *England's Hour*
(303) Harold Nicolson, *Diaries and Letters* (Entry 15th August 1943)
(304) *New Statesman*, London Diary (14th October, 1939)
(305) Mass Observation, *War Begins at Home*
(306) *Daily Telegraph*, (27th May, 1940)
(307) J. B. Priestley, *Postscript* broadcast (11th August, 1940)
(308) Mass Observation, *War Factory* (1943)
(309) Charles Graves, *Londoner's Life* (Entry 7th December, 1941)
(310) Sam Goldwyn, quoted Harry Hopkins, *The New Look* (1963)
(311) Mass Observation, *War Begins at Home*
(312) *News Chronicle* (21st November, 1941)
(313) Margery Allingham, *The Oaken Heart*
(314) *Observer* (1st November, 1970); Lord Goodman reviewing Asa Briggs, "The War of Words" in Vol iii of *History of Broadcasting*
(315) *Tribune* (16th June, 1944)
(316) William Temple to Sir Cecil Graves (15th January, 1943), quoted in *Some Lambeth letters*
(317) J. L. Hodson, *Through the Dark Night* (Entry 13th April, 1940)
(318) C. E. M. Joad, *New Statesman* (22nd August, 1942); article "Prospect for Religion"
(319) Jane Gordon, *Married to Charles* (1940)
(320) Ed Murrow, *In Search of Light* broadcast (30th August, 1942)
(321) William Temple to C. F. Garbett (February, 1944), quoted *Some Lambeth letters*
(322) Harold Nicolson, *Diaries and Letters* (Entry 11th June, 1942)
(323) Speech at Sword of the Spirit meeting (10th May, 1941)
(324) *Sunday Express* (27th February, 1944)
(325) Mass Observation, *Vengeance* (1944)
(326) *Hansard* (9th February 1944)
(327) Arthur Harris, *Bomber Offensive*
(328) Lindemann minute to Churchill (30th March, 1942)
(329) P. M. S. Blackett, *Studies of War* (1962)
(330) *Hansard* (9th February 1944)
(331) Harris minute to Churchill (3rd November, 1943)
(332) C. P. Snow, *Science and Government* (1960)
(333) P. M. S. Blackett, *Brassey's Annual* (1953); article "Recollections of Problems Studied 1940-45"
(334) *Science in War* (1940)

(335) P. M. S. Blackett, *Studies of War* (1962)
(336) *Science in War*
(337) *Evening Standard* (11th October, 1940)
(338) Mass Observation, *Puzzled People*
(339) Speech at meeting in City of London (10th December, 1942)
(340) *Hansard* (2nd December, 1942)
(341) *Economist* (1st May, 1943)
(342) *Times* (19th August, 1940)
(343) Beveridge Report, Cmd. 6404, (1st December, 1942)
(344) I.T.M.A. broadcast (December 1942), quoted Ted Kavanagh, *Tommy Handley*
(345) *Hansard* (17th February, 1943)
(346) Harold Nicolson letter to Vita Sackville-West (3rd December, 1942)
(347) Major Guy Kindersley letter to William Temple (1st July, 1943); quoted *Some Lambeth letters*
(348) *New Statesman*, London Diary (12th December, 1942)
(349) *Economist* (20th February, 1943)
(350) Cecil Beaton, *The Years Between* (Entry 16th July, 1943)
(351) I.T.M.A. broadcast (5th August, 1943)
(352) Evelyn Waugh, *Unconditional Surrender* (1961)
(353) Harold Nicolson, *Diaries and Letters* (Entry 15th September, 1943)
(354) *Partisan Review*, George Orwell's "London Letter"
(355) J. B. Priestley, *Postscript* broadcast (28th July, 1940)
(356) John Pudney, *Dispersal Point and other Air Poems* (1942)
(357) Francis Williams, *What are We Waiting For?* (1941)
(358) Winston Churchill's speech to Miners' Unions representatives (14th October, 1943)
(359) Broadcast (21st March, 1943)
(360) *Economist* (15th January, 1944)
(361) Broadcast (26th March, 1944)
(362) *Ibid*
(363) Report of Director General of Emergency Medical Service (August, 1939)
(364) P.E.P. broadsheet, No. 222 (30th June, 1944)
(365) *Times* (27th December, 1940)
(366) White Paper on A National Health Service, Cmd. 6502 (February, 1944)
(367) James Mackintosh, *The Nation's Health* (1944)
(368) *Ibid*
(369) White Paper on Employment Policy, Cmd. 6527 (June, 1944)
(370) *Economist* (3rd June, 1944)
(371) *Economist* (10th June, 1944)
(372) Broadcast (26th March, 1944)
(373) *Tribune* (4th August, 1944)
(374) *Hansard* (25th January, 1944)
(375) *Daily Express* (21st April, 1943)
(376) Broadcast (26th March, 1944)
(377) Vera Brittain, *Testament of Experience*
(378) Ed Murrow, *In Search of Light* broadcast (30th April, 1944)
(379) Vera Brittain, *Testament of Experience*
(380) J. L. Hodson, *The Sea and the Land* (Entry 26th May, 1944)
(381) Shirley Joseph, *If their Mothers only Knew*
(382) Harold Nicolson, *Diaries and Letters* (Entry 11th June, 1944)
(383) Ursula Bloom, *War isn't Wonderful* (Entry 15th June, 1944)
(384) *New Statesman*, London Diary (8th July, 1944)
(385) Freya Stark letter to Isaiah Berlin (21st June, 1944), quoted Freya Stark *Dust in the Lion's Paw* (1961)
(386) Harold Nicolson, *Diaries and Letters* (Entry 13th August, 1944)
(387) *Ibid* (12th September, 1944)
(388) *Ibid* (10th March, 1944)
(389) *New Statesman*, London Diary (1st July, 1944)
(390) J. L. Hodson, *English Family*
(391) *New Statesman*, London Diary (30th December, 1944)
(392) Ed Murrow, *In Search of Light* broadcast (8th May, 1945)
(393) *Picture Post* (19th May, 1945)
(394) John Lehmann, *I am My Brother*
(395) Raymond Mortimer letter to Harold Nicolson (19th July, 1945)
(396) Ritchie Calder, *New Statesman* (8th March, 1941)
(397) Address to A.G.M. of National Federation of Building Trade Employers (24th January, 1945)
(398) Broadcast (4th June, 1945)
(399) Lord Moran, *Winston Churchill* (1966)
(400) John Lehmann, *I am My Brother*
(401) Lord Keynes paper to War Cabinet (14th August, 1945)

Picture Credits

Index

127